praise for *saving*

Relatable. Fresh. Freeing. *Saving the Saved* is a brilliant book that reminds us of the truth that we are in need of a Savior, not a system. If you have ever felt like you can't be good enough or can't check off enough boxes, then you need to read this book. The gospel doesn't restrict us; it frees us!

Louie Giglio, pastor of Passion City Church, founder of Passion Conferences, and author of *The Comeback*

Bryan Loritts is a highly gifted communicator of grace. This book can be your next step into a more grace-filled life.

John Ortberg, senior pastor of Menlo Church and author of *All the Places to Go*

Meritocracy has crept its way into our culture, our churches, and if I'm honest, at times into my own life and ministry. I'm so glad my friend Bryan Loritts has given you and me a biblically rooted escape from our never-ending quest to equate who we are with what we do. I need to keep rereading this book.

Kara Powell, PhD, executive director of the Fuller Youth Institute and coauthor of *Growing Young*

The wonderful and often forgotten good news for Christians is that Jesus' *last* words on the cross, "It is finished," are also the *first* words spoken over us as we begin our lives with Him. Everything we need in order to secure God's approval, Jesus has secured *for us* through his life, death, burial, and resurrection. When our hearts and imaginations are attuned with these realities, we gain the power to serve God, knowing we are already loved, versus slaving out of fear that we might not be loved. In this masterfully compelling, deeply pastoral, and sorely needed book, Bryan Loritts leads us toward a freedom that, in Jesus, is already ours.

Scott Sauls, senior pastor of Christ Presbyterian Church in Nashville, Tennessee, and author of *Jesus Outside the Lines* and *Befriend*

Bryan Loritts is one of the most thoughtful and biblical leaders I know. In *Saving the Saved*, he cuts to the heart of what the gospel is all about, offering good news not just to sinners but to the self-righteous as well. A freeing and engaging book.

Jon Tyson, founding pastor of Trinity Grace Church, New York City

If you're looking for a commentary on Matthew's gospel that exegetically deep dives into the theological abyss of the former tax collector's version of the life of the Man whose call led him to leave his business profession, put this book down. If you're looking for an investigative journey into the practicality and profundity of the power of pure, performance-less love, welcome to the ride!

Kenneth C. Ulmer, DMin, PhD, pastor-teacher of Faithful Central Bible Church, Los Angeles

If you're a perfectionist and workaholic like me and have struggled to be embraced by grace, this is the book for you. *Saving the Saved* invites us to move beyond our addiction to self-reliance and swim anew in the ocean of God's unmerited love. Bryan Loritts reminds us there is freedom from a salvation-economy of meritocracy into the marvelous gospel of grace.

Rev. Dr. Gabriel Salguero, president of the
National Latino Evangelical Coalition

If your faith feels more like duty than joy—and no matter how much you do for God, it never seems to be enough—then this book is for you. In a fresh, relevant, and authentic style, Bryan Loritts helps those of us who are driven, performance-oriented Christians to experience the rest, freedom, and love God longs for us to share. I wish I had read this thirty years ago.

Chip Ingram, teaching pastor of Living on the
Edge and author of *True Spirituality*

Saving the Saved isn't so much a book as a window giving a direct view into the heart of the gospel. On page after page, Bryan Loritts shows us that on our best day we all need the same thing: grace! He paints a brilliant picture of what it means to trust God with our failures and our successes. *Saving the Saved* is an absolute must-read!

Albert Tate, founder and lead pastor of
Fellowship Monrovia (California)

saving
the
saved

saving the saved

→ HOW JESUS SAVES US ←
FROM TRY-HARDER CHRISTIANITY
INTO PERFORMANCE-FREE LOVE

BRYAN LORITTS

ZONDERVAN®

ZONDERVAN

Saving the Saved
Copyright © 2016 by Bryan Loritts

Requests for information should be addressed to:
Zondervan, 3900 Sparks Dr. SE, Grand Rapids, Michigan 49546

ISBN 978-0-310-34494-0 (ebook)

Library of Congress Cataloging-in-Publication Data

Names: Loritts, Bryan C., author.
Title: Saving the saved : how Jesus saves us from try-harder Christianity into
    performance-free love / Bryan Loritts.
Description: Grand Rapids: Zondervan, 2016.
Identifiers: LCCN 2016011029 | ISBN 9780310344995 (softcover)
Subjects: LCSH: Grace (Theology) | Salvation—Christianity.
Classification: LCC BT761.3 .L67 2016 | DCC 234—dc23 LC record available at
    http://lcnn.loc.gov/2016011029

Cover design: Tim Green / Faceout Studio
Interior design: Kait Lamphere

First printing July 2016 / Printed in the United States of America

To Sunday afternoons in "The Wood"—
Alexis, Howie, Stan, Jody, Al, Marc, and Derek.
We met a lifetime ago,
with the best of intentions and locked arms,
holding one another up in our weakest moments.
Those arms are still linked.
Thanks for not letting me go.
And to my godfather, Bishop Kenneth Ulmer,
for showing me a performance-free love.

Contents

PART 3: LIVING IN AND REFLECTING GOD'S PERFORMANCE-FREE LOVE

introduction

REVOLUTION AGAINST THE MERITOCRACY: THE SURPRISING WAY OF JESUS

I'm not so sure when I became a Christian, although I can tell you when I said the prayer. I was four years old and had just been horrified by a film on hell at vacation Bible school. So over dinner that evening, I told my Christian parents—who also served as pastors—that whatever hell was, I wanted no part of it, and I bowed my head while my father led me in the sinner's prayer. I prayed with the earnestness of a small business owner on the brink of extinction who was betting his savings at the local casino in hopes of making tomorrow's payroll. Not the best way to begin a relationship, but that's how it started. To me, God was someone to be afraid of, not someone to be loved and longed for. I imagined God a little like Tina Turner's former husband, Ike—given to violent mood swings. Calm one moment and wrathful the next. So I became like Tina, walking on eggshells, never feeling as if I was really loved by God and trying to do everything just right, because who knew when "Mount Elohim" might erupt?

And so off God and I went, where the next several decades were spent swinging wildly from one extreme to the other. I was filled either with legalistic pride over my performance and rule keeping or with devastating shame when I would fail. I never knew real peace or joy, and I was tormented by the question, "Am I a genuine follower of Jesus?" It seemed as if my self-esteem was congruent with my performance or lack thereof.

The concepts of abiding and acceptance had yet to penetrate my heart. I knew God had said to Jesus, "This is my Son, whom I love; with him I am well pleased" (Matthew 3:17), but I didn't know he said it to me as well. These were dark times.

Things began to change some years ago when I navigated our church through a four-year study on the gospel of Matthew. One of the first things I picked up on was the group to whom Matthew wrote his gospel: the Jews. I saw myself among these moral people who tried with all their might to keep the rules. They went to synagogue every week, worshiped in the temple, offered sacrifices, gave significantly, and immersed themselves in God's Word. For all of this and more, I found it startling that Matthew would write his gospel to these very moral people. Isn't this like a novice offering to help LeBron James with his defense or Kenny G with his saxophone playing? But the novice was no novice; it was God veiled in human flesh, offering us a completely different operating system of living.

A gospel written to moral people more than implies a difference between the gospel and being moral; it shatters any notion of earning or performance and offers hope and relief. Each week over the course of our four-year journey, I found myself comforted and inspired, no longer walking gingerly around God, but approaching him boldly. An unhealthy fear of God began to dissipate, and I started to realize the ridiculousness of judging who I was by what I did or did not do. It started to hit me: If anything I ever do of eternal value is because of God's grace, and if anything I ever do that brings shame is covered by God's grace, where is the boasting? Where is the shame?

I had been striving for so long, and it wore me out. I was trying so hard to get out from under my dad's shadow, trying so hard to earn respect and admiration on my own merits.

Here's what both you and I have figured out by now: The

kingdom of this world is a meritocracy. It esteems those who have earned the most and performed the best. We are enamored with people's educational résumés, athletic prowess, and trophy cases. We measure people's worth by the size of their churches, number of championships won, and albums sold. And in a social media age, I can actually quantify my performance based on how many followers I have and likes I get.

I have a hunch you can relate to this. What's behind our obsession over grades or working out? Why do we incessantly check social media, especially after we've posted something? Why do we have to go from relationship to relationship, or end up feeling devastated when we are alone? And why does any type of failure launch us over the precipice of grief into a sustained free fall into the valley of shame? Straight-A students with chiseled bodies, people with seven-digit followers on social media, those who are romantically involved with others, those who make tons of money—these are probably some of the most unfulfilled people on the planet. It's possible to ace everything and still come up empty.

There just has to be another way.

It's one thing to talk about our world being a meritocracy; it's a pretty devastating thing to say this is what the church has become. If success in the church isn't measured by the world's standards (money, looks, etc.), we've just replaced one choreographed set of steps for another in our effort to perform. Over the course of this book, we will address the issue of moralism, which is not only seen in the world but has also crept into many of our churches—this notion of adhering to a certain set of external regulations to extrapolate any sense of worth and self-esteem. Sure, the metrics may be different, but the process is the same—trying to gain approval by performing. The church has become a meritocracy. It was never meant to be this way.

JESUS AND THE MERITOCRACY

This idea of a performance-oriented worldview we call a meri-tocracy is nothing new. In fact, in Jesus' day, it was a lot more palpable. Jesus lived in a society entrenched in a caste system where the boundaries of class were clearly defined. To the Romans, success in life was based on money, citizenship, caste, and family. Rich never mingled with poor, and women were mere objects. The truly successful were wealthy married men who enjoyed a harem of women and had several sons.

It's almost laughable when you think it was into this context that a poor, single, chaste, childless, homeless Jesus entered. What's more, Jesus didn't even attempt to find meaning by the rules of the Roman meritocracy. Nothing in the gospels would point to him going through the Ivy League rabbis of his day. He didn't seek wealth or a wife. His circles defied the clearly defined boundaries of the meritocracy. Jesus conversed with both the wealthy and the poor. He enjoyed rich friendships with both men and women. He stood before both Roman government officials and blind beggars. Jesus was comfortable enough in his own skin to have a prostitute rub his feet at a party hosted by extremely con-servative religious leaders. And when offered the chance to move from his "cubicle" to the "corner offices" of the world, he politely turned down the "promotion." Jesus refused to be crowned king before his time and even had to be pestered by his mother to per-form his first miracle. Speaking of miracles, he routinely told his beneficiaries to keep quiet. I mean, there is absolutely nothing in the gospels that would remotely suggest Jesus was trying to prove himself or gain significance and approval from others. Jesus was many things, but he was never a performer.

Parenting has a way of exposing where you really stand when it comes to the meritocracy. Believe me, Korie and I know.

We have three sons, and we genuinely try to parent from the basic default of yes unless there's a really good reason to say no. We try. Sometimes this puts us into some pretty dicey scenarios.

We grew up in an era where what you wore to church really mattered and, according to some, was a sign of worship to God, though I've yet to find that verse. I vividly remember wearing a three-piece suit in the middle of August in Atlanta at a church with no central air-conditioning, where we were handed fans with a wooden stick and a piece of cardboard stapled to it with a picture of Dr. King on one side and an advertisement for a funeral home on the other (I really did feel like dying). I nearly suffocated in my act of "worship." With my feet dangling off the pews that hot summer day, I promised if I was ever blessed with kids, they would never have to dress up to go to church. So when our boys got old enough to dress themselves, we let it be known they could wear whatever they wanted. Whatever. We'd bite the knuckles on our index fingers on Sunday mornings as our creative middle son would come barreling down the stairs with plaid shorts and a striped shirt. Our youngest could always be counted on to wear some sort of basketball jersey, athletic shorts, high tops, wristband, and one of those athletic sleeves that go on the arm but because his arms are so thin it slumped down like a grandmother's oversized stocking. And our oldest would dress okay; he'd just never give a thought to deodorant or showering. Korie would shoot me a "say something" look while I'd shoot back that "honey, you know we made a promise" look. Then we'd get in the car and pull up to the Southern church I pastored, and our kids darted across the parking lot to go to youth group, completely comfortable in their own skin, while the nice Southern parishioners looked at my kids with consti-pated smiles on their faces as they waved hello.

Sometimes I envy this about my kids. Do you know the grief

I would catch preaching in a headband and a Stephen Curry jersey? Can you imagine how repulsed people would be when they caught a whiff of my natural self as I draped my arm around them for prayer at the altar?

But my kids couldn't care less. I know at some point it'll hit Myles that he should probably not wear stripes with plaid. There will be a moment when Quentin will see the value in a daily shower followed by a dab of deodorant, and Jaden—well, something tells me he'll want to be married and buried in an athletic jersey. Our kids are relaxed and confident in who they are and give little thought to conforming to the values of our society. This will change, but when it does, it will be a sad day.

By the sheer way in which he lived, Jesus unleashed an assault on the meritocracy and its invitation to live a performance-driven life. In fact, Jesus even said unless we come with the posture of children, we can't experience life in the kingdom (Matthew 18:3). Just as my kids pay little attention to the traditional church fashion sensibilities of their day, so we cannot participate fully in the kingdom of heaven while keeping in style with the kingdom of this world. Jesus is calling us to a richer way, one that is not dependent on what you do but on who he says you are.

And we are God's children with whom he is well pleased. It's as simple as that.

ETERNITY IN OUR HEARTS

There's another reason it's time to kick the meritocracy to the curb.

The thing about the performance-based life is that it often assumes this life is all there is. But deep down, we know there's more—and we're hungry for it.

That's why people feel empty, even when they have the meritocracy made.

Just look at King Solomon.

I once heard a clinical psychologist muse that if she had to render a diagnosis on the person writing the biblical book of Ecclesiastes, she would say he was clinically depressed. For all of his wealth, women, and wisdom, the author, Solomon, was unsatisfied. He longed for more. This longing is exposed not only when he exhaled, "Everything was meaningless, a chasing after the wind" (2:11), but also when he pointed out that God has "set eternity in the human heart" (3:11).

Why was Solomon depressed as he wrote his memoirs? Because what he had acquired in this life didn't quite scratch him where his soul itched. There was a longing in him that nothing in this life seemed to satisfy. His frantic grasps for meaning revealed a yearning for more.

Statistics today underscore Solomon's ancient quest for more. In his classic book titled *Heaven*, Randy Alcorn reveals, "The sense that we will live forever *somewhere* has shaped every civilization in human history . . . The unifying testimony of the human heart throughout history is belief in life after death. Anthropological evidence suggests that every culture has a God-given, innate sense of the eternal—that this world is not all there is."[1] What Solomon expressed went beyond the bounds of incurable optimism and set a cornerstone for what it means to be fundamentally human—an unrest with this life, coupled with the pervasive feeling that there must be more; a longing to rest in something or someone eternally transcendent, to feel in our guts we've been accepted and have found performance-free meaning. To deny such heavenly impulses is fundamentally inhumane.

Quoting Friedrich Nietzsche, psychiatrist Viktor Frankl wrote, "He who has a why to live for can bear with almost any how."[2] Frankl was able to affirm such a profound assertion because of his personal experience as a prisoner of the Nazis in the early 1940s. Through the suffering he himself experienced and also witnessed among fellow Jews at the hands of the Nazis, he pondered the question of why some prisoners could navigate the horrors of life in the death camps with hope and joy, and others could not. Essentially, Frankl was interested in why the spirits of some were indestructible and others were not. He concluded that what was at stake was not the how—their circumstances. They had no control over their situations or surroundings. Instead, if they were going to rise unbroken from their situation, Frankl theorized they had an all-encompassing why. There was something at play within them that refused to have their spirits held hostage to what was outside of them.

You may not be in a death camp, but if you've been leasing time on this earth long enough, you know what it's like to experience your own version of heartache. Maybe it's fertility challenges. You entered holy matrimony assuming you would have biological children. Now it's been several years and countless trips to the doctor, and you're still dealing with a barren womb and a broken heart. Or maybe you know the pain of having your heart shattered by the one you entrusted it to. Or maybe it's some addiction that continues to plague you, and you're at the end of your rope, wondering if you'll ever be free. You may have lost a child or a loved one. The examples are endless.

My wife and I have been there. Hurt has come to our address, sure it has. There have been cancer scares, miscarriages, surgeries, financial difficulties, marriage pressure, betrayal from people we thought were friends, and more. Plenty of times we've wanted to throw up our hands and quit. What's gotten us through the hows of hard times has been the why of life—and that's something no amount of trophies can offer. Because sure, a knockout performance feels great in those moments when life is good. We can bet Solomon enjoyed his palaces, feasts, and building projects, at least for a little while. But when tragedy comes knocking, what good are gold stars and straight A's?

To find the "why" for living that holds up under pressure, we have to go deeper.

THE INDESTRUCTIBLE ONE

Our longing to emerge from life's hardships unbroken is at the core of being human. What I want to explore is not so much this global longing, but the path to get there. Exactly how do we live performance-free lives when we've been culturally conditioned to find approval in the meritocracy of this world? How does one emerge from the pain of divorce without wallowing in shame, spending his or her life trying to do good things to make up for the tragedy? How does one find some semblance of security in their relationship with God while battling a porn addiction? How in the world do we endure the hardships of life without giving up on God, without feeling that God has given up on us? And when life is going so well, how do we keep a healthy distance between who we are and the successes we enjoy?

The writer of Hebrews says something striking about Jesus Christ. Writing to recent converts to Christianity, he tells them, "This becomes even more evident when another priest arises in the likeness of Melchizedek, who has become a priest, not on the basis of a legal requirement concerning bodily descent, *but by the power of an indestructible life*" (Hebrews 7:15–16 ESV, emphasis mine). In referencing Jesus Christ, the writer says he lived an indestructible life.

As the author of Hebrews begins his letter, he has a daunting task on his hands. His recipients have just come to faith, and not long after their conversion, all hell breaks loose. According to Hebrews 10:32–39, many had been thrown in jail, others had their property confiscated, and still others were beaten and bloodied. These new converts were doing the math: Since following Christ, their lives hadn't been materially enriched; instead, things had gotten worse. Assessing their postconversion carnage, some had even wondered, *What did I do wrong?*

Some of us can relate, can't we? Since following Jesus, maybe your business has headed financially south, your marital stress has spiked north, and your kids have ventured out west to the proverbial far country in rebellion. Maybe like the Hebrews, you've taken out your calculator and deduced that following Jesus Christ has not been all you thought it would be, and just maybe, like the Hebrews, you're doing your own internal audit, scouring for some bad thing you did to deserve all this.

Let me shoot you straight. This book is not about how to have earthly happiness while sprinkling a little Jesus on top. The indestructible, performance-free life is not about using Jesus as our cosmic concierge so we can live lives of economic prosperity and ease. The abundant life that Jesus came to offer is something that transcends bank accounts and a clean bill of health. The performance-free life is a life centered on Jesus Christ in which we refuse to have our joy tethered to the external events of life or to our personal strivings to measure up. The performance-free life looks to the Indestructible One, Jesus Christ, as our sole source of strength who, when we had no hope of performing our way into God's good graces, performed *for* us by dying on the cross and rising from the grave. Through *his* performance, Jesus became the Indestructible One who offers us the performance-free life that no one can take away. To borrow from Viktor Frankl (who borrowed from Friedrich Nietzsche), it is Jesus Christ—not ambition, perfection, money, or relational status—that becomes our *why* for living.

THE WHY FOR LIVING THAT TRANSFORMS

Some time ago, I had the honor of meeting and getting to know one of my heroes in the faith, Joni Eareckson Tada. At the age of seventeen, she dove into the Chesapeake Bay—into water she thought was a lot deeper than it was. Her tragic miscalculation rendered her paralyzed for life. While for most people, depression and disability would seem synonymous, for Joni, her devastating "how" has not incarcerated her spirit or pilfered her joy. To know Joni is to see an enigma wrapped up in a riddle. Her wheelchair and immovable limbs suggest she should be depressed, perpetually beating herself up for this mistake. Yet her smile, otherworldly joy, and melodic voice that sings praise to our Maker leave one scratching their heads. How has she been able to do it? Joni walks with the Indestructible One, Jesus Christ, and as a result, she rests in his performance-free love for her. She found a why for living that has transformed her devastating how.

You want this. I want this. That's why we're making our way to the gym, embarking on another diet, and trying with all our might to make better moral choices. Maybe these acts of discipline are the longings of our heart to find acceptance and approval. If we could only get down to a certain weight, kick that bad habit, or give it everything we have in order to finally fulfill the elusive "New Year's Resolutions" list, then maybe, just maybe, we'll feel better about ourselves as we work our way up the meritocracy. I wish you the best as you attack the treadmill or StairMaster. (Me, I'm going to the elliptical—my knees just can't take the pounding of the treadmill!) But in our quest to reform our bodies, let's not forget our overall lives. We need something that will transcend our workouts, and that someone is the Indestructible One, Jesus Christ. The only One who can free us from the rat race of constantly trying to measure up.

This book is an invitation to participate in the revolution against the meritocracy. So if you're ready to fire your inner lawyer—who is constantly cross-examining you, pointing out your deficiencies in an effort to get you to perform more—and instead look to Jesus, who offers you a better way of living, a performance-free kind of living that will hold up under all of life's pressures, then this book is for you. Using Matthew's biography on Jesus' life as our guide, each chapter of this book will examine an episode from the gospel of Matthew and show how Jesus waged war against the meritocracy as he stands with arms open wide, beckoning us to rest in him.

I hope you'll join me in resting in the arms of Jesus, who longs to whisper to us what God said to him at his baptism: "This is my Son, whom I love; with him I am well pleased."

what goodness isn't

soul songs

THE LIFE YOU'VE ALWAYS WANTED

Then Jesus was led by the Spirit into the
wilderness to be tempted by the devil.
Matthew 4:1

The question of performance-free love transcends ethnicity, gender, and socioeconomic status. "Am I forever loved for who I am?" is the background elevator music to our hearts. And if such a love does exist, how does it manifest itself in my life? The answers to these questions are found in Matthew 3 and 4.

The slaves of the antebellum South ached for something more. In a world where they were treated as less than human, they knew what others said about them, and the way they were treated was at odds with who they were created to be. Listen to the songs they sang in the sweltering heat of Southern plantation cotton fields, and you will get a peek at their unsettledness. Sure, some of their songs were encrypted messages of escape passed through the vocal highway of melody, but their songs carried a richer message. Frederick Douglass, the great nineteenth-century abolitionist orator, reveals why the slaves sang:

I have often been utterly astonished, since I came to the north, to find persons who could speak of the singing, among slaves, as evidence of their contentment and happiness. It is impossible to conceive of a greater mistake. Slaves sing most when they are most unhappy. The songs of the slave represent the sorrows of his heart; and he is relieved by them, only as an aching heart is relieved by its tears.[1]

The slaves sang because something was wrong. Life as they knew it was amiss. Like a CT scan, the songs of the slaves revealed the most intimate sections of their hearts. At their core, the slaves sang because they longed for more. Their songs articulated the deepest aches of their souls.

The biblical equivalent to the old Negro spirituals is a collection of psalms called laments. Journey through these lament songs, and you hear the aches of the Jewish people, who put pen to the disequilibrium in their souls. These laments could easily be mistaken for Negro spirituals, as the Jews wondered if they were loved, if God really cared about them—and if he did, would he protect them from their enemies? Embedded in the Jewish laments and Negro spirituals are universal questions that continue to play on the iTunes playlists of our hearts.

Like the oppressed Jews and African slaves, we all want to know we're valued and esteemed for who we are and not for what we do. We want a performance-free love infusing us with inherent worth and dignity. We need to know we're valued and accepted, even when our performance fails. Does such a thing even exist? And if it does, what does it look like?

PERFORMANCE-FREE LOVE

There is a beautiful episode in the life of Jesus where we see him receive performance-free love. In Matthew 3 and 4, Jesus is on the precipice of his public ministry. In just a few moments, he will pick his disciples and ascend a mountain to preach the greatest sermon ever preached—the Sermon on the Mount

(Matthew 5–7). But when we encounter Jesus in in these early chapters of Matthew, he's still considered some average "Joe" whom hardly anyone knows, from some Podunk village called Nazareth. The timing of this scene is critical, because remember, he's yet to perform. He's worked no resurrections, extended no forgiveness, stilled no storms. In Matthew 3 and 4, Jesus is just what many mistakenly think him to be—a mere human born under suspicious circumstances.

It's in this context that we hear God say to his yet-to-perform Son at the end of Matthew 3, "This is my Son, whom I love; with him I am well pleased" (verse 17). Remember the time Jesus turned a few pieces of fish and loaves of bread into an all-you-can-eat buffet? Yeah, God says these words way before then. And there was a time when Jesus brought back to life a dead Lazarus. Yep, God spoke these words before then too. What about when Jesus died on the cross and rose a few days later? God told his Boy he was proud of him before all of that. At the end of Matthew 3, God simply says to his Son, "I'm proud of you." Period. This is performance-free love, and the same God who says to his Son, Jesus, "This is my Son, whom I love; with him I am well pleased," speaks these words daily over us, inviting us to go from striving to abiding.

What happens next is no mere coincidence. Right on the heels of receiving his Dad's performance-free love, Jesus is led into the wilderness to be tested by Satan in what has been called the three temptations of Jesus—and the undercurrent to each temptation is Satan beckoning Jesus away from his Father's performance-free love and inviting him to prove himself by turning stones to bread, commanding his angels to miraculously deliver him, and worshiping Satan. What Satan wants is to engage Jesus in the biggest fight of his life, and it's a fight between resisting or resting in his Father's love.

Jesus' fight is ours. Every day, we must choose between resting in God's performance-free love for us or striving to find acceptance in the meritocracy of this world by our own efforts. The same evil one who beckoned Jesus to prove himself by doing celestial magic tricks invites us to prove ourselves through over-work, fear-driven control, obsessing over our bodies or grades, and a whole laundry list of other things. Each of these, and more, is but the whispering of Satan, begging us to turn stones into bread.

Not only do all three temptations have a common theme of performance, but Jesus' rejection of them also shows us what a person who is experiencing God's performance-free love looks like. We know we're resting in God's performance-free love when we have a future hope, an unshakeable love, and a transcendent purpose.

A FUTURE HOPE

Satan's first temptation of Jesus seems rather innocuous—just turn some stones into bread. Jesus' refusal sends a strong message that what Satan is offering is out-of-bounds. I find myself perplexed by Jesus' refusal. The text suggests that Jesus is at the end of his fast, so what's the harm in turning some stones into bread, especially when you don't have to run to the grocery store to get it?

Jesus' response to Satan's door of opportunity reveals the harm: "Man shall not live on bread alone, but on every word that comes from the mouth of God" (Matthew 4:4). The phrase "bread alone" unlocks the reason for Jesus' reticence: Satan wants him to focus exclusively on the here and now and contract spiritual amnesia when it comes to the eternal. "Live for the moment, Jesus, and forget about eternity" is what Satan is after. Jesus' refusal to prove himself to Satan by living for the here and now not only reveals that he's resting in his Father's love, but it also betrays where his hope lies.

The problem with life is that it can be oh-so-daily. Is it just me, or does it seem like the natural default is to become so obsessed with this life that we forget about the next? Those who live this life with their sights set on the life that is to come are those who are resting in their Maker's love. How we perceive eternity affects how we view and navigate the present. If this life is all there really is, then we may as well join with the rich land-owner of Luke 12 who examined his crops and concluded that he should eat, drink, and be merry, for tomorrow he may die.

History has shown a correlation between what we think about the future and the choices we make in the present. The twentieth century has been called by many historians the blood-iest century in history. From the gas chambers of Auschwitz to the killing fields of Cambodia, man's capacity to do mass, irrep-arable harm to his fellow neighbor defies imagination. Many of the leaders of these killing regimes did not hold to a future hope. Their Darwinian philosophy of the survival of the fittest caused them to toss caution to the wind.

But, some may ask, how do we explain the cruel chapter of American slavery that was perpetrated at the hands of so-called Christians who believed in heaven? Slaves were deemed to be soulless. So with no future hope for a slave, who cared how they were treated? They could be kicked, berated, or shot like one's dog or ox.

I know these examples are extreme. You're probably not masterminding some mass murder, so what does this have to do with you or with your coworker in the cubicle next to you? Everything. If there is no future hope, then there is no divine accountability, and if that's the case, why would anyone sub-scribe to any sort of moral standard? What's the point? Engage in as much sexual pleasure as you desire, commit "socially acceptable" acts of injustice (I'm guessing you don't want to go to jail), and spend or hoard money to your heart's satisfaction while giving no thought to the needs of the less fortunate. I mean, really, what's the point if there's no future hope?

Some years ago, I was approached by a young man in our church who described himself as an "unfulfilled atheist." He wanted to know why he should consider Christianity. I responded by asking him if he could name any of history's atheists who had done a lot of good for their world. Unable to answer me, I gently dove in. I pointed him to Peter Claver of Columbia, who cared for slaves and built leprosariums. I talked of William Wilberforce and the Clapham Circle, the small community of men and women most responsible for leading the charge to dismantle the slave trade. We dialogued about William Booth and his care for the poor, and then about George Müller, one of the leaders of England's nineteenth-century orphan care movement. I reminded him that the civil rights movement of the mid-twentieth century that gained rights for African Americans like me was led by a courageous cohort of Christ followers.

The point of my history lesson was not to shame him but to show how all these individuals, and more, not only cared deeply for their community and bettered their world, but they did so from the moral base of a Christianity that believed in a future hope. Their conviction that this world is not all there is fueled their frantic labors to right the very present wrongs done to slaves, orphans, and the poor. These, and many others like them, declined the opportunity to "live on bread alone."

Performance-free love does not mean we do nothing to help others. I mean, just think of Jesus, the One who heard God say how proud he was of him. It's next to impossible to read a single chapter in the four gospels without seeing him feed, heal, or comfort someone. Jesus showed kindness to a woman caught in adultery. He healed a paralytic. He did dinner with the social pariahs of his day. Jesus did more than preach; he cared—and along the way, he left the world a better place. What drove his labors? He was not just convinced of a future hope; he came from and embodied this future hope.

Refusing to "live on bread alone" revolutionizes how we see and approach life. Our future hope, arising out of a performance-free love, doesn't make us passive or indifferent; just the opposite, it inspires us to do all we can do to help better our present world. I remember having dinner with a well-known actor who loves Jesus and refuses to "live on bread alone." During our meal, I asked him if there was a role his Christian convictions would not allow him to play. With a smile on his face, he shook his head no. Curious, I proposed what I thought to be some compromising roles—a killer, sex addict, pedophile. He responded by saying he sees the Bible as a redemptive story of great conflict between good and evil, with good winning out in the end. He is convinced every film is crafted from the same recipe of conflict and in some way gives a picture of the gospel. If this is true, he reasoned, someone has to personify evil. There needs to be a kidnapper, an unjust boss, a philandering husband. Then pausing for effect, he said, "Bryan, the only role I could not accept is one where evil wins." The projects he signs up for must have a future hope.

I left our dinner inspired. A future hope touches not only actors and screenwriters but also landscapers, stay-at-home moms, teachers, and people from all walks of life. A future hope challenges the notion that a job is just about money or personal career advancement. A future hope pushes against the paradigm that life is all about my personal happiness. A future hope offers fresh, new ways of parenting and relating to one another. Yet because our future hope is anchored in a performance-free love, our labors are not done *for* God's (or anyone else's) approval but *from* his approval.

A future hope inspires me. Refusing to "live on bread alone" means there really is nothing that happens in this life that is final. I have a family member who clings to this message. After years of prayer and scores of conversations centered around what it means to follow Jesus, she said yes to his performance-free invitation. About a year later, this recent Christ follower was diagnosed with cancer. The prognosis does not look good at all, and we've shed some tears, and are praying for God's healing. That's our hope. But we have a greater hope. As my friend Matt Chandler—himself having been afflicted at one time with cancer—says, "We're all terminal." Should Christ linger in heaven, there will come a day when death will knock on our door. But if we have been adopted into the family of God (Ephesians 1), no form of cancer, heart disease, or ailment has the final say. In words that soothed a grieving friend, Jesus said, "I am the resurrection and the life. The one who believes in me will live, even though they die" (John 11:25). A performance-free love has a future hope.

AN UNSHAKEABLE LOVE

Satan is undeterred by Jesus' denial to "live on bread alone." So he goes and opens another window of opportunity.

Then the devil took him to the holy city and had him stand on the highest point of the temple. "If you are the Son of God," he said, "throw yourself down. For it is written:

'He will command his angels concerning you,
    and they will lift you up in their hands,

so that you will not strike your foot against
a stone.'"

Matthew 4:5–6

Like the runner Harold Abrahams, who exhaled before a race,
"I will raise my eyes and look down that corridor, four feet
wide, with ten lonely seconds to justify my whole existence,"[2]
Satan once again wants Jesus to validate himself to him. He asks
Jesus to give a private performance to justify his existence, to
prove his identity. Jesus will have none of it. He simply replies,
"Do not put the Lord your God to the test" (Matthew 4:7). Jesus
knows who he is—the Lord God. He doesn't need to perform
like Harold Abrahams in order to affirm his worth.

Where does such security come from? Remember the words
of Jesus' Father: "This is my Son, whom I love; with him I am
well pleased." Before Jesus turned water into wine, stilled a
storm, or raised the dead, Jesus' Papa said he was proud of him.
God's words are so helpful to me as a father of three sons. Our
kids need to hear me say, "I'm proud of you. You are my beloved
son, and I'm really pleased with you," regardless of the grades
on a report card, the failure to take the trash out (again), or the
number of turnovers in a basketball game. God's Son was able
to turn down Satan's request to perform because he knew he
was intrinsically loved by his Father. Jesus emerged unscathed
from this temptation because he felt the security of being loved
for who he was, not for what he did.

We all ache for this unshakeable love, and without it, we
find ourselves on a collision course with misery. Think about
celebrities. These great performers were never constructed
to bear the crushing weight of deity. With each concert, film,
television show, or album release, they're asked to justify their
existence, to prove their worth. And when the record label drops

them, the crowds dwindle, or the offers slow to a halt, many find it impossible to cope, because the song in their soul is for an unshakeable love.

If I could pinpoint the most miserable of the miserable, I think it would be comedians. There's something to the irony of so many comedians dying tragic deaths. Those with a special gift to make the masses laugh are among the most tormented. Jim Belushi, John Candy, and Chris Farley all died way too young. The suicide of Robin Williams took our collective breath away. And when we heard he was depressed, the irony was too obscene. Comedians getting depressed?

Among the world's beloved comedians, Richard Pryor's life may well have been the most tragic. He never heard from his father anything close to what Jesus heard from his. Richard's dad told him he would never amount to anything. His mother was a prostitute who worked for a time in the brothel that Richard's grandmother owned. Richard recalled how he'd watch his mother disappear into a bedroom, and then he'd peer through the keyhole to see her turn another trick with some stranger. You may wonder why little Richard Pryor was in a brothel in the first place. It happened to be his home.

Seeking validation, Richard soon discovered he had a penchant for making people laugh, so he took to the stage. Those who knew his upbringing understood that the ninety minutes he performed each night was therapy. Every laugh he drew out from the audience was an attempt to feel loved. When the last joke was told and he relinquished control of the microphone, his straining for love continued. Richard was notorious in his abuse of women. Any woman who thought of leaving him or expressed any kind of attention for another man was met with violence. Richard knew the pain of a mother who abandoned him and a father who despised him, so he vowed not to allow himself to be abandoned again. The quest for love led him to abuse substances that permitted him to momentarily mute the soul's song of being loved intrinsically. His life was one long lament in which he never quite found the love he so desperately needed.

The actor Kevin Costner hinted at this kind of longing in his moving reflections of Whitney Houston at her funeral. One of history's great singers shared Richard Pryor's penchant for drugs, a habit that, in the words of Michael Jackson, would cause her to be *gone too soon*. Costner recruited Whitney to costar with him in the film *The Bodyguard*. When the two met for a screen test, Whitney was nearing the height of her powers. Yet when she was running late for the test, Kevin found her tucked away in a dressing room, gazing deeply into the mirror, wondering aloud if she was pretty enough and if Costner thought people would love her.

I bet Whitney's questions sound familiar to you because you've asked some of the same ones. A woman who has been living for an extended time with her boyfriend maybe feels as if sex has become a perpetual audition, quietly hoping to perform her way into an engagement ring. You may be overworking out of a deep fear that failure to perform on your job will result in more than the loss of a paycheck—in the abdication of your identity. Even as a pastor, I find myself overly obsessed about a poor sermon, speculating that my failure to perform will mean people will start leaving my church. String together enough of these sermonic whiffs, and maybe I too will be out of a job. In our own ways, we join the company of Whitney Houston by wondering if we're "pretty enough."

It's here that the life of Jesus and the gospel offer great comfort. If you want to understand the Bible and God's inexhaustible love for you, you should get to know the Hebrew word *chesed*—a word used more than two hundred times in the Bible. One hundred twenty-six of those times are found in God's iTunes playlist called the Psalms.

Scholars struggle with how to translate *chesed*, because there's really no equivalent. The best some translators can come up with is "steadfast love." *Chesed* is God's unfailing, unrelenting, un-quitting love (to make up a word). *Chesed* is a love that never gives up, never gives out, and never gives in. The heartbeat of *chesed* is covenant, and when God makes a covenant with his people, he never divorces. *Chesed* is a performance-free love.

King David spoke most often of *chesed*. Of the 126 times the word is used in the Psalms, many of those usages come from his hand. For example, Psalm 63 describes a time when the bottom has fallen out of David's life. His own son Absalom has recruited David's close friend Ahithophel to help mastermind a coup d'état. With his life in danger, David flees Jerusalem, crosses the Kidron Valley, and hides in the wilderness of Judah. With a little bit of time on his hands, David cries out to God, and the transcript of his anguish is Psalm 63. In the middle of his prayer, he declares that God's steadfast love (*chesed*) is better than life (verse 3). God's unfailing love for David provides the needed ballast for his turbulent soul.

Scholars call 2 Samuel 7 the Davidic Covenant—the moment when God enters into *chesed* with David, telling him that his throne will be established forever. God made good on his word by sending his own Son, Jesus Christ, who came from the lineage of David: "Of the greatness of his government and peace there will be no end" (Isaiah 9:7). But what blows my mind is that God enters into covenant with David in 2 Samuel 7, and four chapters later, David eyes a woman named Bathsheba, knowingly commits adultery with her, and then tries to cover up his mess by having her husband killed. Talk about Bed Bath &

Beyond! I say this is mind-blowing, because God is omniscient (all-knowing). So when God made a covenant with David, he knew that just a little while later, David would put on a terrible performance and break his heart.

As the New Testament begins, God offers his people a new covenant. The same *chesed* that bound a holy God to an adulterer is offered to you and me through Jesus Christ. Romans 5:8 describes the New Testament equivalent of *chesed*: "God demonstrates his own love for us in this: While we were still sinners, Christ died for us." This verse is rich with theological truth, but the one word that brings me to my knees is *while*. God didn't wait for me to get cleaned up before he loved me. Instead, he saw me as is, loved me as is, and saved me as is. Performance-free, unshakeable love.

I don't know how blemished your spiritual credit report may be. Chances are, when you glance in the rearview mirror, you'll see some things you're not proud of. Maybe you've had an abortion. Someone else reading this could be dealing with a divorce caused by your betrayal. Or maybe you are mired in materialism, basing your self-esteem on the latest fashion, all the while wondering if you're "pretty enough." The good news of the gospel is that God sees you as is and wants you as is. It bears repeating: "God demonstrates his own love for us in this: While we were still sinners, Christ died for us."

Put it this way. Imagine I barge into your wedding ceremony just as you are about to exchange vows. I motion to the tech guy in the back to press Play, and to your astonishment, on the big screen in front of the scores of people who have gathered for your beautiful day, I show your betrothed (and the whole church) all the awful things you have done, are doing, and will ever do to break his heart. He's devastated as the tears begin to cascade down his face. But to our amazement, he still wants to marry you. So he grabs your hand, gazes into your eyes, and says, "I do." That's *chesed*. That's Romans 5:8. That's performance-free love. That's the kind of love the One who made us offers.

A TRANSCENDENT PURPOSE

Denied for the second time, Satan opens one more door. He takes Jesus to a high mountain, shows him all the kingdoms of the world, and says, "All this I will give you . . . if you will bow down and worship me" (Matthew 4:9). How does Jesus keep from laughing? He's being offered something he already owns.

In exchange for his ludicrous proposal, all Satan wants from Jesus is the currency of worship. Jesus responds, "Away from me, Satan! For it is written: 'Worship the Lord your God, and serve him only'" (Matthew 4:10). Having swung and missed for the third time, Satan leaves.

You want to know what swag is? It's a person walking in his or her God-intended purpose, and no one had more swag than Jesus. He could confidently turn down the opportunity to own the world, not only because it was already his, but also because he knew who he was and what he was here for, and he felt completely secure in his Father's performance-free love. How do you and I know we're marinating in God's performance-free love? We're resting and walking in God's purpose for our lives.

Jesus knew his purpose was to worship God. The critical word here is *worship*. Satan longs to be the focal point of Jesus' worship, but Jesus shakes his head and says the only One worthy of worship is God. We were created by God to worship him only.

To worship is to ascribe worth to an object or a person; it is to say through words and actions that a particular thing or person is valuable. Because of this, the Bible connects closely the concepts of worship and glory. *Glory* means "weight." In antiquity, the value of something could only be determined by how much it weighed. You placed an item on scales, and the heavier the thing was (glory), the more it was worth (worship).

It is important to tie together the themes of glory and worship when we think about our purpose. Jesus did. Just hours before he experienced the brutality of the cross, Jesus stole away to pray. In John 17, he reflects on his time here on earth, and in great satisfaction exhales, "I have brought you glory on earth by finishing the work you gave me to do" (verse 4). In his work, Jesus displayed the glory of God.

The apostle Paul had a passion to invite Christ followers to display the infinite glory of their Creator in all of their pursuits. To the Corinthians, Paul wrote, "So whether you eat or drink or whatever you do, do it all for the glory of God" (1 Corinthians 10:31). Centuries later, the Westminster Shorter Catechism openly wondered what man's chief end is. Mining the Scriptures, they retorted, "To glorify God and enjoy him forever." You and I were designed to worship God by displaying his eternal weight in everything we do. We know we're living the performance-free life when no matter what our activity is, we find a way to show off God by giving him glory.

Jesus knew this. Why else would he stand on a mountain overlooking all the kingdoms of the world and turn down Satan's offer without any thought? It wouldn't surprise me if this scene was emblazoned on Jesus' mind when he said some time later, "What good will it be for someone to gain the whole world, yet forfeit their soul?" (Matthew 16:26). There's an itch in our souls that no amount of power, position, or prestige can satisfy.

But why was Jesus' life ordered around the worship of his Father? Why was Jesus so obsessed with glorifying God that he endured the pain of the cross? Because he knew the daily euphoria of his Dad's performance-free love. And what should drive you and me, who have been made in the image of God, to honor our Papa? Because he loves us unconditionally.

If we really stopped to consider God's crazy, unshakeable love for us, we would be overwhelmed with gratitude. And where there's gratitude, there tends to be an earnest quest to express thanks through acts of honor and glory.

This is why the question of work is so profound. Have you ever wondered why you are here—what your purpose is? Sure you have. You may be feeling the pressure to declare a major or to make a career change or position shift within your organization. How do you decide? Or how do we help our kids discern what to do with their lives? These are more than just good questions; they're songs in our souls.

In wrestling with these very questions in my own life, I've returned many times to God's conversation with Moses. In Exodus 3 and 4, God offers Moses a career change. For forty years, Moses has been leading sheep, and now God wants him to lead his people. God invites Moses to travel to Egypt and tell Pharaoh to let Israel go. Overwhelmed by the prospect, Moses declines, giving a list of reasons he thinks should disqualify him. Irritated with Moses' obstinacy, God asks him what is in his hand. Moses inspects the instrument he's holding—the one that had served him well for the past forty years in leading sheep—shrugged his shoulders, and said, "It's a staff." God then tells Moses to throw down this familiar object, so he does—and it turns into a snake. "Pick it up," God says. So Moses grabs it by its tail, and it turns back into a staff. In convincing Moses of his new purpose, God simply uses what is in his hand to point him in the right direction.

When God created you, he gave you a staff—he put something in your hand. Your staff represents your gifts and passions. There's not a single person alive who wasn't born with a staff.

If you have questions of purpose, begin by taking inventory of what's in your hand. What are your gifts and passions? What is it that when you do it, you're encouraged by others to do it again? What activity do you engage in where time just seems to fly? What's in your hand?

Korie and I were playing cards with some friends with a documentary about the horse-racing, Triple Crown winner Secretariat playing in the background. When the film came to the part where Secretariat wins the Belmont Stakes by a record-setting thirty-one lengths, our game stopped, and it felt as if we were in a moment of worship. Our friend said she thought she just caught a glimpse of God. Watching Secretariat lap the field that day, you got the feeling that this is what God made him to do. Secretariat wasn't created to haul dreamy-eyed couples around in some carriage; he was made to run.

Can you imagine Muhammad Ali trading stocks, or Steve Jobs boxing? You got the sense as you watched Ali throw a jab, or even now as you may hold one of Steve Jobs's products, that these things were what they were made to do. Punches and creativity are in their hands.

My parents obsessed about helping me discover what was in my hand. So I played the viola, took acting classes, and sang in the choir. I sang so loud and so bad that my mom ended my tenure in the church choir almost before it began. She determined that singing just wasn't in my hand. I enjoyed sports but wasn't great, so when I announced at season's end that my baseball career was over, there were no arguments from my folks. Looking back, I'm grateful for parents who didn't try to force something that wasn't in my hand.

At seventeen, I preached my first sermon to a packed Sunday evening audience. In hindsight, it wasn't the best sermon—not even a good one—but the people were gracious and encouraged me to keep at it. Getting in the car, I felt a sense of euphoria. I *had* to do it again. So I told my father—an accomplished preacher—that this is what I wanted to do with my life and asked him to help. During the next few years, he tutored me in preaching and showed up when he could to hear me, offering support along the way. He saw what was in my hand and did his best to nurture the "staff." Every time I stand before a group of people with an open Bible, I can't help but feel what we felt as we watched Secretariat run: This is what I was created to do.

My ten-year-old son loves basketball—I mean *loves* it. When he was five, we found him in my study entranced by a documentary on the game where Wilt Chamberlain scored a hundred points. On school mornings, he inhales his breakfast so he can shoot a few baskets before it's time to go. I've seen this kid work on his free throws in twenty-degree weather. I'll spare you the typical dad talk about how great his son is—even though he's averaging about twenty points a game in his league for ten-year-olds! Basketball seems to be in his hand, and it will be fun to see what God does with his passion for the game.

But Jaden needs to know that basketball is a means to a greater end—to display the glory of God. If I could play a little with Paul's words, I'd tell my son, "So whether you eat or drink *or play basketball*, do it all for the glory of God." If basketball were ultimately about paychecks and fame, it would be like Jesus standing on the mountain overlooking the kingdoms of the world and accepting Satan's offer to worship him.

We know what was in Jesus' hand. While brain surgeon Dr. Ben Carson has been said to have gifted hands, his had nothing on Jesus'. The Son of God's hands turned water into wine, stilled storms, and fed thousands from a few pieces of fish and loaves of bread. In Matthew 9, we see the hands of Jesus giving strength to once-dead legs in front of a watching crowd.

When this former paralytic walked, the crowd was "filled with awe; and *they praised God*, who had given such authority to man" (verse 8, emphasis mine). This is the point of purpose—displaying God's glory through our gifts and passions to a watching world so that God is worshiped.

Steve Jobs once invited the world-famous classical musician Yo-Yo Ma to play in his home. When the cello player finished, Steve Jobs was mesmerized. Like the crowds who praised God when Jesus healed the paralytic, Jobs said to Yo-Yo Ma, "You playing is the best argument I've ever heard for the existence of God, because I don't really believe a human alone can do this."[3]

One of the greatest evidences for God is work done well. When our gifts intersect with our passions, we have purpose, and our purpose is to display the glory of God.

What does the performance-free life look like? When you and I live with a future hope, rest in an unshakeable love, and walk in our God-created purpose, we are living the performance-free life.

And I think you'll find that this kind of life has some swag.

CHAPTER 2

my jesus mercy

WE ALL STAND IN NEED OF GRACE

Al Capone, the most notorious gangster in American history, had these three words etched on his tombstone: "My Jesus Mercy."

If you're like me, there's something in you that says, "Yeah, Al, you *better* ask for mercy." Given the many people he gunned down and the number of women he slept with, people he bribed, and laws he broke, a request for mercy seems more than appropriate. Someone once said that when we get to heaven, we will be surprised on two fronts. We will be surprised at who isn't there—those we thought for sure would be there but who aren't. And we will also be surprised at who is there—those we thought for sure would not be there but who are. If I have Al Capone as a next-door neighbor in heaven, I will be shocked, shouting, "My Jesus Mercy." I'm going to go out on a limb and guess you're probably thinking the same thing. The odds of Al being in heaven are very slim.

We assume Al didn't make it into the pearly gates because, well, he did bad things. And the fact that Al did a *lot* of bad things, more than he did good things (or so we think), means Al didn't make it in. Heaven is for good people; hell is for bad people—or so the story goes. But Jesus, and particularly the gospel of Matthew, paints a much different story. The Jesus presented by Matthew would suggest that Al isn't the only type of person deserving of the epitaph "My Jesus Mercy." You and I may want to give some thought to having these words written on our grave markers as well.

AN INSULTING GOSPEL

God approved four biographies on the life of Jesus—we call them gospels: Matthew, Mark, Luke, and John. Each of these documents presents a different aspect of Jesus while forming a composite picture of God's only Son. The uniqueness of each gospel is so striking that God wanted four definitive biographies documented on his Son for all of time.

One question worth asking when we sit down to read a gospel has to do with audience: Whom is this specific book written to and why? Determining the audience helps us in how to understand and apply the specific truths of the given gospel. For example, Matthew writes his biography of Jesus to the Jews. Think about it—Matthew writes his gospel to the Jews. Read that sentence again, because it's loaded with innuendo, some of which is insulting.

Jews in Matthew's time were as moral a people as it got. They attended the synagogue every week. They went to the temple on high and holy days to celebrate and offer sacrifices. Many Jews had memorized the first five books of the Bible (yep, that would include the book of Leviticus). And you would have to look long and hard to find a group of people more generous than the Jews. Some scholars believe the average Jew gave around 20 percent of their annual income to God and the poor. This doesn't seem to be the kind of crowd an author would need to address about the person of Jesus and the performance-free love he came to offer. I mean, if anyone could earn their salvation, it would be these folks! But that's not how it works.

The undercurrent in Matthew's gospel is a message that

his three contemporaries emphasize as well: Jesus is the only One who can offer a life rich with meaning and transcendent purpose, a life filled with unconditional love and acceptance. The punch line for Matthew and his contemporaries is that they want their audience to be convinced of the person and work of Jesus Christ so they will turn from their sins and be ushered into the kingdom of God.

All four biographers also give special attention to the pious Pharisees, a sect of Jews who were perceived as the poster children for goodness and morality. Yet all four biographers highlight the constant friction that took place between Jesus and these morality police, pointing out that it was Jesus who was the standard of goodness, not the varsity side of "Team Good"—the Pharisees. While the Jews were hardly perfect, when compared to others, they certainly had a leg up in the "good" department. So the fact that Matthew writes his gospel to the Jews is the epitome of irony. It would be like us trying to give Tom Brady lessons on how to be a good quarterback or writing a letter to Charles Spurgeon on how to preach, or like a star on a TV reality show offering acting lessons to Denzel Washington. Wait a minute—a whole book on how to live a good, meaningful life addressed to the Jews? Are you kidding me?

But the fact that Matthew writes his biography to moral Jews is both ironic and insulting. It has been said that grace insults our sensibilities. Therefore, if the indestructible life is based only on Jesus and his gracious offer of salvation, then all of us, even the morally upright, should consider ourselves insulted. In his own way, God wanted to send the precise message that Al Capone wasn't the only one deserving of the epitaph "My Jesus Mercy." Synagogue-attending, Scripture-memorizing, temple-worshiping, 20-percent-giving-to-God-and-the-poor people who die without Christ in their lives should also consider having Al

Capone's words written on their tombstone. "My Jesus Mercy" is not just for the so-called bad; it's also for those esteemed as "good."

MY JESUS MERCY

So as Matthew dips his pen into ink and writes across the papyrus, he has one objective in mind: convincing "good people" they are just as much in need of the mercy and grace of Jesus Christ as "those bad people." If you're looking for one episode in the gospel of Matthew that gets at this point of moral people needing the mercy of Jesus in order to rest in his performance-free love, look no further than Matthew 19:

> Just then a man came up to Jesus and asked, "Teacher, what good thing must I do to get eternal life?"
>
> "Why do you ask me about what is good?" Jesus replied. "There is only One who is good. If you want to enter life, keep the commandments."
>
> "Which ones?" he inquired.
>
> Jesus replied, "'You shall not murder, you shall not commit adultery, you shall not steal, you shall not give false testimony, honor your father and mother,' and 'love your neighbor as yourself.'"
>
> "All these I have kept," the young man said. "What do I still lack?"
>
> Jesus answered, "If you want to be perfect, go, sell your possessions and give to the poor, and you will have treasure in heaven. Then come, follow me."
>
> When the young man heard this, he went away sad, because he had great wealth.
>
> *Matthew 19:16–22*

If ever there was a person who was the prototype for success in the meritocracy of our world, this guy was it. This was a man who thought he could save himself all on his own. He was labeled as rich—someone who had "great wealth." He was young, with more mileage on the road of life in front of him than behind. And if this wasn't enough, he hadn't forgotten God, because the story tells us he had done his best to keep the Ten Commandments. But for all of his wealth, youth, and morals, he was unfulfilled, a truth betrayed by his opening question: "What good thing must I do to get eternal life?" His question is astounding, because for all of his attempts at doing good, he still asks for another helping of morals in an attempt to soothe his disturbed soul. The rich young man's question underscores the whole premise of Matthew's gospel: Gritting our teeth and trying harder to be good in order to find meaning can never bring the satisfaction our souls long for.

THE MORALIST'S MISSING LINK

Close your eyes and listen to this man's plea. It has every bit the feel of consternation. There's not a smile or a tinge of joy in his request. I've learned over the years that joy is rarely in the DNA of the moralist or legalist. I can say this with confidence because it takes one to know one. I'm the oldest of four siblings who grew up in a Christian home in which both of my parents are still married and consistently modeled what it means to follow Jesus. Like Matthew's audience, I was in church every Sunday, taught to give generously to God, and warned against the evils of sin. Somewhere along the line, I bought into the fallacy that Christianity came down to what I did and didn't do. So to feel good about myself, I not only needed to perform more, but at the same time, I needed to be within close proximity of those who weren't "as good as me." C. S. Lewis was right: In order for pride to exist, there must be comparison with what we would deem to be an inferior other.[1]

It started out innocent enough—wanting to win the sword drills and memory verse competitions at vacation Bible school. Later on, it was showcasing what little knowledge I had of the Bible by theologically sparring with my Sunday school teacher. Oh how I loved asking him for his interpretive opinions on such complex biblical texts as Hebrews 6 or on the curse of Ham. This so-called good, moral kid had the gift of playing devil's advocate. Then at the age of seventeen, I decided to become a preacher. My home church immediately put me up to preach on a Sunday night in the spring of 1990. I cringe at those early sermons—not only because they were the epitome of awful, but also because the worst thing you can do is give a blooming moralist a microphone, especially at the age of seventeen. So I blasted away and beat up the people by putting on them what Francis Schaeffer called "the cruelty of utopianism."[2] I preached a perfect standard (which is what we *should* be doing), but the punch line was moralism: Try harder, white-knuckle it, stop doing that, start doing this. As if that wasn't bad enough, what made things worse is the fact that the people I was preaching to loved it, for they too were of the moralism fraternity, and that only encouraged my spiritual malpractice.

And so I continued, but along the way, I found myself being weighed down by the crushing burden of this impossible stand-ard. Like the Jews, I had syllabus shock when it came to God's Word and his requirements of me. There was just no way I could keep at it. While I expounded on the evils of sin, I had this nag-ging sense in the back of my mind that I was never good enough. My momentary efforts at being good never gave me lasting joy. Like the rich young man in Matthew 19, I was becoming more and more empty and confused; and like him, the only thing I knew to do was to ask for another helping of "good works."

I'm sure you can relate. In the early 2000s, a number of young religious teenagers were surveyed to find out what they believed about God and life. The research concluded that an overwhelming majority believed in a worldview called Moralistic Therapeutic Deism—an approach to navigating the world that says, (1) God exists; (2) he wants us to be happy; and (3) the way to happiness is by doing good things.[3] These teenagers believe in God and some sort of a righteous life; they just think the way to get there is by taking the moral road, by asking for another round of good deeds. Like the young man in our passage, they say in their own way, "What good thing must I do to get eternal life?"

Can't you see that Matthew 19 exposes the problem with Moralistic Therapeutic Deism? This rich young man has spent just about all of his life doing good, but when we meet him, he's not really happy (the second tenet of MTD). He's suffocating under the pressure of "good." There is no joy for those who venture down the moral road, because enough is never enough.

MEASURING MORALITY

Jesus' answer to this depleted man is one of the most brilliant responses ever rendered: "Why do you ask me about what is good?" Jesus replied. "There is only One who is good" (Matthew 19:17). Our English word *good* comes from the Old English word that simply means "to be like God." This is exactly how Jesus applies the word *good* in our text. Here this man asks for another helping of "good," thinking he will get yet more commands, but instead Jesus points him to a person—to God.

In Mark's biography, he adds a little wrinkle to this exchange between Jesus and this rich young man:

> As Jesus started on his way, a man ran up to him and fell on his knees before him. "Good teacher," he asked, "what must I do to inherit eternal life?"
>
> "Why do you call me good?" Jesus answered. "No one is good—except God alone."
>
> *Mark 10:17–18*

In Mark's account, the man calls Jesus good, prompting Jesus to reply that only God is good. Jesus' response is a head-scratcher. Is he saying *he's* not good? Is he not God? Just the opposite. When Jesus tells this man who calls him good that it is only God who is good, it is a genius affirmation of his deity. Jesus is saying *he is God*. What's more, as God, Jesus is the standard of good.

This is important to remember as we return to Matthew's version of the story. If Jesus is the definition of what's good, then this changes everything when it comes to our search for unconditional, performance-free love. We all want a life rich with substance, value, and significance, something that reverberates beyond the grave. The trick is not in our aspirations to find this kind of life but in the route we take in trying to get there. The most common path we venture down is the path of moralism. Be a good boy or a good girl, and you'll get there—or so we think. Treat people nice. Be faithful to your lover. Give some money to those in need. Be spiritual. Don't defraud others. If you're nice and good enough, then you'll get there. But the dilemma becomes this: If Jesus is right when he tells this rich young man that he (Jesus) is the standard of good, then pro-scribing more good to do won't solve this man's dilemma. This is probably one of the hardest truths to digest.

I wasn't the best student in middle school, which means I failed my share of tests. Now whenever this would happen, I would stand outside the classroom and conduct my own Gallup Poll. As my classmates filed out, I asked over and over, "What did *you* get?" You know why I asked this question? I was anxious to see if everyone did as bad as me, because if they did, then the teacher would have to grade on something called "the curve." The curve is not reality, but it is necessary when, for example, everyone fails an exam, and so the teacher adds points to the test scores, and what was once an F can quite possibly become a B. The result of all this leaves us with a distorted view of reality. Sure, I could boast in having a B, but truthfully, I *had* failed. Needless to say, I loved the curve.

Inevitably, though, there would be some know-it-all I'd want to take to a corner and lay hands on (and not to pray), because not only had he failed to fail the test; he aced it. Thanks to this little Einstein, my curve was ruined, and I had to live with my failing grade.

Take Jesus out of the picture, and humanity's "classmates" become the standard for goodness. If Jesus is not on the scene, then I can measure my goodness based on what I do or don't do. If Jesus isn't in the mix, then there's boasting in my sexual purity, charitable giving, and the number of people I helped this week. In this scenario, thank God there are people like Jerry Sandusky who will always give me an inflated view of myself, allowing me to believe I'm good.

But the problem with all of this morality stuff is that we're using the wrong standard. What got Jesus nailed to the cross is being that know-it-all kid who aced the test everyone else had failed, thereby ruining our curve. In his own humble way, Jesus says, "You're not the standard; I am." What he says to the rich young man he says to all of us: "You don't need another helping of good in order to be good; instead, you need to come to the only Good One and surrender your life to him, and you will be good" (which, by the way, is good news for Jerry Sandusky and others we are tempted to brand as awful). There is no goodness outside of the indestructible Jesus Christ.

As familiar as this rich young man was with the Scriptures, I don't know how he missed the point that he could never do enough good things to be accepted. God said through the prophet Isaiah, "All of us have become like one who is unclean, and all our righteous acts are like filthy rags" (Isaiah 64:6). Will you think about that for a moment? On your best days, when you are in the Word, praying, boldly sharing your faith, and generously giving to the needy, without Christ, independent of him, God calls those deeds "filthy rags." Bummer.

In Psalm 16—another passage this young man probably heard preached in one of the many synagogue assemblies he attended—David writes, "I say to the LORD, 'You are my Lord; apart from you I have no good thing'" (verse 2). I mean we haven't even made it to the gospels or Paul yet, and there it is, right in front of our noses, in flashing lights: "There is no goodness apart from God."

TWO ROADS

There are two ways to react to the truth that there is no good apart from God. Either we can be momentarily insulted, deny the truth, and continue on in our journey to do more "good" things. Or we can allow humility to bloom in our souls, casting ourselves on the mercy of the only good one—Jesus Christ. For me, every day is a fight to choose the latter, because there's a freedom in knowing I don't have to do good things to experience God's unconditional love.

If we decide to take the former path, pride and self-righteousness will soon come. We see this in the rich young man.

Jesus baits him by telling him to keep the Ten Commandments. The young man responds by saying he has kept them. Do you see the arrogance? The Ten Commandments represent a comprehensive ethical code. Break one, James tells us, and you break them all (James 2:10). None of us can keep the very first commandment—you know, the one about having no other gods before the one true God—because all sin is idolatry. But here is this young, confident man saying that when it comes to the Ten Commandments, he is batting a thousand. His request for more good to do is akin to him saying, "Jesus, the Ten Commandments aren't enough; you got some extra-credit ones to add to the list?"

Before we too quickly judge this man, who among us hasn't done something similar? I've given myself a hug while looking at my annual giving report. On numerous occasions, I've whispered a "thank heaven" when a couple whose marriage is on life support just left a counseling appointment by yours truly. I've looked at some porn addicts the way my wife looks at insects, wishing they would move on and get it together. Oh, the self-righteousness! Each of these instances, and more, puts me in the company of this arrogant rich young man, who says in so many words that the Ten Commandments aren't enough; he needs more. I'm surprised this man's arrogance didn't ignite Jesus' anger.

THE MIRAGE OF MORALITY

In his own way, I guess Jesus does erupt. His quiet frustration with the man's pride takes on the form of a well-articulated argument that backs this young man into a corner he has no hope of getting out of.

To paraphrase,

Jesus: So, you've kept all the commandments, have you?

Rich Young Man: Sure have [with a smile on his face],
    especially the ones that have to do with loving your
    neighbor.

Jesus: Oh really? Okay, tell you what, just go, sell everything
    you have, and give to the poor; then you can follow me.

Rich Young Man: [Blank look on his face. Long pause.
    Deep sigh.]

"When the young man heard this, he went away sad, because he had great wealth" (Matthew 19:22).

The Ten Commandments can be divided into two sections. The first set of commandments have to do with our relationship with God: We're not to have any other gods before him or take his name in vain—you know, things like that. The last part of the Ten Commandments is concerned with how we relate to others—to our neighbors: We're to honor our parents, not commit adultery, and so on. If you notice, the specific commands mentioned in Matthew 19 are the horizontal ones, the commands about how we treat our neighbors. These are the ones the rich young ruler says he's especially aced.

Now look at the challenge Jesus gives him. It's as if he says, *So if you've really aced the horizontal commands, which are all about loving your neighbor as yourself, let's see how much you really love your neighbor. Sell all of your possessions and give to the poor.* The gauntlet has been thrown down. He has a choice to make: love my neighbor and fulfill those commands I'm sure I've aced, or place myself and my money above people. His exit reveals he's not as moral as he has portrayed himself to be. His morality is only a mirage. Given the opportunity to love his neighbor at the expense of himself and to follow Jesus, he chooses to love himself and bask in his riches.

Social media can create a mirage of the perfect life, elevating envy in a person's followers. A kid may post pictures of himself on Instagram enjoying the once-in-a-lifetime vacation, but rarely, if ever, will we see photos of him in trouble, eating a very average dinner, or having a bad day. In the digital age, social media affords us the opportunity to be the star of our own reality show, where the proverbial camera is always on our good side.

This bit has been going on for millennia. We have the habit of announcing our good deeds, while keeping the lid tightly closed on our bad ones, creating a veneer of morality. While the jury is still out on Bill Cosby (if it even convenes), we were all shocked at the onslaught of allegations levied against him. None of us imagined Heathcliff Huxtable, America's perfect dad, was even capable of being accused of such things. We were just as surprised about the child abuse allegations hurled at Michael Jackson and infidelities of Tiger Woods. While *Selma* director Ava DuVernay masterfully handled the marital indiscretions of Dr. Martin Luther King Jr. in her film, there was no avoiding the avalanche of questions my kids had, as their image of the civil rights leader was tainted.

And while we're in the naming business, throw yourself in there as well (along with me). We are all complicated messes, and the point of all these historical examples is not to demonize anyone but to show that when we know the lights are on and the cameras are flashing, we will always present an incomplete picture. Like the rich young man, when asked to give ourselves a grade, we have the habit of giving ourselves higher scores than we deserve, unwilling to admit we deeply need God to grade on a curve. We all need mercy.

FINDING GANDHI

Jesus' last words to this morally confused young man offers a helpful paradigm in how to see morality: "If you want to be perfect, go, sell your possessions and give to the poor, and you will have treasure in heaven. Then come, follow me" (Matthew 19:21). Our story begins with this man asking Jesus what he needed to do to get eternal life, and it ends by Jesus answering him.

There's a false teaching called antinomianism, which is a big confusing word that means "without the law." Like staring at one's reflection through a mirror that distorts everything, antinomianism has an erroneous view of grace. To antinomians, there is little to no need for good works in the Christian life—just believe in Jesus, follow him, and everything will be okay. Well, these persons should cut Matthew 19:21 out of their Bibles, because Jesus commands this man to actually do something: sell what you possess. Later, in another conversation between Jesus and a wealthy person (Luke 19:1–10), we see the grace of God invading Zacchaeus's heart. He says he will give half of his possessions to the poor. Zacchaeus's unsolicited gesture prompted Jesus to affirm his faith by saying that salvation had come to his house that day. When God saves us, he doesn't just change our motives and desires; he transforms our actions as well. Doing good and following Jesus go hand in hand. It's just that we don't do good to be accepted; instead, because we are accepted, we do good. We'll chat more about this later.

Jesus' challenge to the rich young man doesn't stop at philanthropy—giving to the poor. He goes on to invite this once wealthy man to follow him. As we read the gospels, we see this word *follow* a lot. The word has the idea of "attachment" and paints a picture of two people being in relationship with each other. Following is relationship; it's the comingling of lives; it's sharing meals, experiences, and the very essence of who we are. Jesus isn't just inviting this man to write checks and give away stuff; he's beckoning him to intertwine his life with Christ's. A lot of people do good things independent of Jesus, but where Jesus insults us is by telling the man that philanthropy isn't enough to get eternal life. He has to be in relationship with the Worthy One, Jesus Christ.

I love Mahatma Gandhi. As an African-American man, I am especially indebted to this quiet revolutionary, because his nonviolent philosophy was an inspiration to Dr. King and became the primary weapon in the civil rights movement of the mid-twentieth century. There's much about the life of Gandhi that should be admired and emulated. But there are also some deeply troubling truths about his life.

In his autobiography, Gandhi tells of the time some Christians tried to proselytize him by giving him a Bible and encouraging him to read it. So straightaway, Gandhi immersed himself in the Scriptures. When he came to the person of Jesus Christ, Gandhi bristled. He said these words:

> It was more than I could believe that Jesus was the only incarnate Son of God, that only he who believed in him would have everlasting life . . . My reason was not ready to believe literally that Jesus by his death and by his blood redeemed the sins of the world . . . I could accept Jesus as a martyr, an embodiment of sacrifice, and a divine teacher, but not as the most perfect man ever born. His death on the Cross was a great example to the world, but that there was anything like a mysterious or miraculous virtue in it my heart could not accept.[4]

There you have it. Gandhi, this incredibly moral man who fasted, prayed, and even abstained from sex with his wife for years because he didn't want to appear as if he was demeaning her, denied that Jesus Christ was God's only provision for man's sin. Gandhi believed he could be free from sin on his own terms, independent of Christ.[5] The crux of the matter is before us: If Jesus says he is the only true repository for good, yet Gandhi believed he could be good outside of Christ, was Gandhi in fact truly moral? Based on his own words, can we really say he was good, independent of Jesus?

NOT ENOUGH

Al Capone isn't the only one who needs the mercy of God. The Bible says Gandhi, Martin Luther King Jr., and other "saviors" need a Savior too. From the preacher to the person who has never darkened a church door, we are all in dire need of mercy. There is no one who can save themselves. This is the disturbing message of Matthew, this gospel written to the Jews. Scripture-memorizing, synagogue-attending, temple-sacrificing, money-giving people are not truly good on their own. Or to say it a different way, being a sexually monogamous, hardworking, giving-to-charity, worshiping-some-sort-of-higher-power person does not make one good. There is no goodness outside of God's only Son, Jesus Christ. This is exactly the message of David in Psalm 16:2: "I say to the LORD, 'You are my Lord; apart from you I have no good thing.'"

Gandhi, me, you—all of us—should give some serious thought to Al Capone's epitaph: "My Jesus Mercy."

a good impossibility

WHY MAN-MADE GOODNESS JUST DOESN'T CUT IT

At the corner of Knight Arnold and Mendenhall Roads—a seedy South Memphis intersection—stands a woman named Jackie. On hot summer days, she walks the streets topless. Don't stare at her, though; she'll hurl the most vulgar obscenities your way. The locals don't pay her any mind. "It's just Jackie being Jackie," they say.

Peering at her through a storefront window one Saturday afternoon, I asked my barber about her story. "Jackie used to be a lawyer who drove a Mercedes and earned well into the six figures," he said. I was stunned. "What happened?" I asked. At a party one evening, she had gotten a taste of cocaine. This one sample opened the levees of desire. Jackie would stop at nothing to get more. She emptied her bank account and then stole from family and friends to support her habit. Now she sells her body to anyone bold enough to endure her eccentricities. A lawyer-turned-cocaine-addicted prostitute. One taste transformed her desires, which influenced her behaviors.

One taste of something powerful can have either wildly negative or positive effects. For Jackie, that one taste sent her barreling down the wrong road. But when we get a real taste of God's amazing love, it has the power to revolutionize all of who we are. This is an otherworldly, unconventional method of change, but it's the only legitimate path we can take to experiencing the way of Jesus and the life of true meaning he offers.

In the Sermon on the Mount, Jesus drills deeply into the total transformation God has in mind for those who have tasted his goodness.

The Sermon on the Mount is one of Scripture's most beloved portions. I remember my high school football coach, who plastered practically nude women on his office wall and could curse with the best of them, having us take a knee before kickoff to recite the Lord's Prayer—one of the most-quoted ancient texts, found in the heart of the Sermon on the Mount. Christians and non-Christians alike have run to this sermon for guidance in making sense of life. But look closely at the Sermon on the Mount, and you'll be disturbed by a lot of what's there.

Trying to keep the ethical demands Jesus makes in the Sermon on the Mount is like asking my four-foot-something ten-year-old to dunk on a regulation basketball hoop. Impossible.

Let's say your middle school child gets his nose bloodied by a bully. Are you really going to say to him, "But I tell you, do not resist an evil person. If anyone slaps you on the right cheek, turn to them the other cheek also" (Matthew 5:39)? And how are you measuring up to this one? "For I tell you that unless your righteousness surpasses that of the Pharisees and the teachers of the law, you will certainly not enter the kingdom of heaven" (Matthew 5:20)? If the apostle Paul is right when he includes adulterers in a list of those who will not experience the kingdom (1 Corinthians 6:9), then men, what do you have to say about this? "You have heard that it was said, 'You shall not commit adultery.' But I tell you that anyone who looks at a woman lustfully has already committed adultery with her in his heart" (Matthew 5:27–28). Impossible. We clearly have some work to do.

THE IMPOSSIBLE IDEAL

Remember, Matthew's biography on the life of Jesus is all about trying to get good, moral people to understand that their white-knuckled, grin-and-bear-it, try-harder attempts to do good can't cut it when it comes to God and his kingdom. The gospel, Matthew argues, is not just for irreligious, never-attending-church people; it's also for religious, church-attending, Scripture-memorizing, keep-your-pants-on people as well. Jesus died not just for the "bad" but also for the so-called "good." Matthew writes his gospel to make sure we understand this truth.

We're reminded of this when we come to chapters 5–7 of Matthew's gospel—the Sermon on the Mount. More than Mark, Luke, and John, Matthew devotes the longest plot of biblical real estate to Jesus' sermon because it is so key to his argument. I can see this former tax collector saying to himself, *This is so good*, as he takes detailed notes while Jesus preaches. In talking about God's unconditional, performance-free love for us, it's important to hang out here for a little bit. What's at stake is not our longing for this kind of life—we all long for it—but the route we take to get there. In the Sermon on the Mount, Jesus both shows the impossibility of man-made goodness and inspires us to lean into him and become awash in his transcendent love.

If you need proof of the impossibility of the Sermon on the Mount, look no further than the myriad of interpretations of Jesus' message throughout history. Through the years, some thirty different interpretations of Jesus' sermon have been given, and that's a conservative estimate. Biblical scholar Leon Morris categorizes these interpretations in two primary colors, with all others being a variation:

A good deal of the discussion turns on the achievability of the ethical teaching Jesus gives here. For some this is an impossible ideal, demanding such a lofty ethical standard that no one can possibly attain it; as a result they dismiss it from the world of practical living. Others view it as something that people can and should attain.[1]

The buffet of interpretations is the result of the unbelievably hard ethical demands of Jesus' sermon. When the sermon concludes and the benediction is given, we're left shaking our heads and trembling on our feet, thinking there's just no way we can do this on our own. And that's the point.

THE HEART OF THE MATTER

When we come to Matthew 5–7, it helps to ask who it is that Jesus is talking to. If you guessed the masses in general, you would be wrong. "Now when Jesus saw the crowds, he went up on a mountainside and sat down. *His disciples* came to him, and he began to *teach them*" (Matthew 5:1–2, emphasis mine). In the Sermon on the Mount, Jesus is having a conversation with his handpicked followers as the crowd listens in. This should help us get our arms around the difficult truths embedded in this message, because the ethical challenges in the Sermon on the Mount are only meant to be lived by those who are in relationship with God. We have no hope of loving our enemies, abstaining from lust in our hearts, or going to war with worry unless Jesus is in the center of our lives.

Jesus said a lot of hard things, and if you were to ask me to come up with a short list of his hardest sayings, Matthew 5:20 would be right at the top: "For I tell you that unless your righteousness surpasses that of the Pharisees and the teachers of the law, you will certainly not enter the kingdom of heaven." If I had been in the crowd listening to Jesus, I would have quietly gone back to work mid-message. As the old preachers used to say, "This ain't no shoutin' sermon." I can feel the silence of the masses as they listen in disbelief.

The Pharisees were perceived as being to righteousness what Academy Award winner Denzel Washington is to acting. They didn't just try to uphold a system comprised of 613 dos and don'ts called the law; they actually came up with *more* laws (mainly Sabbath laws)! They were known for their long prayers in public, debates over the nuances of Scripture, and tithing with metronome consistency. Speaking of the Scriptures, they memorized the Torah—the first five books of the Bible. The Pharisees were also moral referees, constantly throwing flags at the slightest violation. And Jesus says that unless we do better, we have no hope of inheriting the kingdom? Okay, I feel encouraged.

Five years ago, my son Myles was diagnosed with hypereosinophilic syndrome (HES). Our eosinophils are an aggressive type of white blood cells. Like a 250 pound linebacker, our eosinophils are warriors waiting to be unleashed on anything that can harm our bodies. Something strange enters our system, and these bad boys attack. In Myles's case, his eosinophils are always attacking—with nothing to fight. As the doctors explained, at some point, our son's HES could turn on his organs and prove fatal. Korie and I were devastated.

"There's no cure for HES," we were told. At best, it can only be managed through steroids, and even with that, we can expect certain seasons when his eosinophils rage out of control. I want my son's HES to be gone. I don't want to manage anything. "No such luck," the doctors told us. Unless something supernatural happens, HES will be as much a part of our lives as our tears.

When Adam and Eve acted independently of God by living life on their own terms, a foreign substance called sin invaded our hearts. Paul wrote that "through the disobedience of the one man the many were made sinners" (Romans 5:19). Sin is a universal problem, posing the biggest hindrance to righteousness and a vibrant relationship with God. If you are in Christ, you share my frustration over sin's presence. We want it gone. I can't wait for the moment when I won't have to go to war with my wayward eyes, selfish desires, and raging ego. I empathize with the apostle Paul, who screamed out, "What a wretched man I am! Who will rescue me from this body that is subject to death?" (Romans 7:24). Like my son Myles, whose blood gets drawn for the umpteenth time to check his eosinophils, what Christian doesn't know the weariness of apologizing for the same sin struggle? We want sin gone as badly as Myles wants to be done with HES.

We can take one of two approaches to our spiritual HES. Often we'll use manufactured human resources to try to manage our sin. Got a porn problem? Find some computer program like Covenant Eyes that will help you stay off certain Internet sites. Greedy? Can't control your spending? Read some Christian financial guru and apply their principles. Having a social media affair? Join an accountability group.

Now don't get me wrong, there is a place for "steroids" like these. We should remember that Jesus suggested to those who couldn't restrain their loins to gouge out their eyes and cut off their hands (Matthew 5:29–30). Two centuries later, Origen (one of the church fathers) took Jesus' words to heart. Unable to control himself, he opted for castration. I sure hope there is another way.

Jesus tells us there is. The righteousness of the Pharisees and the teachers of the law was external and outward. In Matthew

6:1, Jesus says these religious leaders did their good deeds to be seen by others. Toward the end of his ministry, Jesus would have some very tough things to say about the Pharisees, calling them whitewashed tombs full of dead people's bones (Matthew 23:27). The image is piercing—they are wonderful-looking tombs, while the inside contains decaying corpses. When questioned about why he and his disciples didn't wash their hands before they ate, Jesus accused the religious leaders of cleaning only the outside of the cup while leaving the inside dirty (23:25). Through all of these pictures and more, Jesus is unmasking a group of people who cared more about appearances than character, about perception than reality. The righteousness of the Pharisees was external, not internal.

Some years ago, Korie and I were invited to speak at a marriage conference. We've done enough of these events to forecast that a fight is looming on the horizon. It's uncanny how it seems that every time we set out to help other people's marriages, ours finds trouble. A few minutes before we had to go to the ballroom, Korie and I got into one of those marital realignment sessions. Okay, it was a very heated argument—over what I don't know. But I do remember having to cut short the argument because we were running late. As we got off the elevator and walked into the room filled with married couples waiting to glean pearls of wisdom from our "stellar marriage," I grabbed my wife's hand and faked a smile, as if to say, "We've got it together." If only you'd seen the look Korie shot me! I wanted to portray an image that we had it together when the reality was that we needed to be sitting among the conferees taking notes.

External righteousness is, at best, plated gold or a wood veneer, where the outside looks good but will never pass the authenticity test. This was the righteousness of the Pharisees. And maybe it's yours as well.

Who hasn't experienced seasons of hypocrisy? Think about it, all sin is a breach of integrity, making all of us, in the words of the old mob wise guys, *fugazis*—fakes, phonies.

The problem with the Pharisees is that their hypocrisy was of the deliberate sort. With steeled determination, they were guilty of false advertising, passing themselves off as the real thing when they were nothing more than a spiritual Ponzi scheme. Unchecked external righteousness is like selling someone ocean-front property in Nebraska. It's spiritual fraud.

IMPOSSIBLY POSSIBLE

As Jesus moves deeper into his sermon, he turns up the heat. Having shocked his audience in Matthew 5:20, their eyes widen even further as he continues:

> "You have heard that it was said to the people long ago, 'You shall not murder, and anyone who murders will be subject to judgment.' But I tell you that anyone who is angry with a brother or sister will be subject to judgment. Again, anyone who says to a brother or sister, 'Raca,' is answerable to the court. And anyone who says, 'You fool!' will be in danger of the fire of hell."
>
> *Matthew 5:21–22*

As if this wasn't enough, he twists the knife: "You have heard that it was said, 'You shall not commit adultery.' But I tell you that anyone who looks at a woman lustfully has already committed adultery with her in his heart" (Matthew 5:27–28).

Who isn't guilty on both counts?

In talking about anger and lust, Jesus begins by appealing to the Ten Commandments. Murder and adultery were understood by all to be physical acts. If you took someone's life or had sexual relations with another person's spouse, you were guilty of murder or adultery. This is how we understand these offenses today. Murder is an external act. Adultery involves two people, not a rehearsed thought.

But this isn't enough for Jesus in his sermon. Having reminded us of the law, he says, "But I tell you." These are rather highly offensive words. Think about it, the Ten Commandments were given to Moses from the mouth of God on Mount Sinai. Every Jew understood these laws to have come directly from God. But now they are listening to a teacher from Nazareth add to the law by saying, "But I tell you." *Wait a minute, am I missing something?* they must have thought. *Only God can amend his laws—adding to or taking from them. Who are you?* The correct answer would be God. The words of Jesus—"But I tell you"—affirm his deity. He is announcing in clear terms that he is more than a carpenter or some skilled teacher. He is God.

This God-Man, Jesus, now moves from the physical realm of the law to the heart. Murder, Jesus teaches, is no longer just the material taking of another person's life; it is the refusal to forgive, a boiling disposition that insults, calls names, and assassinates the relationship. Adultery isn't just sexual intercourse; it's the lingered look, acting out the immoral scenario in vivid scenes on the stages of our imaginations. Sin is not just outward, but inward—a matter of the heart.

And it's here that we have a major problem in our journey to experiencing God's performance-free love. I can control my actions at least for a season, but my heart? This seems impossible. And if Jesus is right—that I can't really control my heart—then do I have any hope of receiving God's unconditional love?

Jesus has led us to a fork in the road. Go the way of outward righteousness, and you may grin and bear it for a while, but at some point, it won't work. Or we can go the other way—the way of Jesus.

Hundreds of years before Jesus stood on a hillside near the Sea of Galilee, God spoke through the prophet Ezekiel of the better way: "I will give you a new heart and put a new spirit in you; I will remove from you your heart of stone and give you a heart of flesh" (Ezekiel 36:26). There it is. God says the new righteousness is not some white-knuckled, grit-it-out behavior modification where I perform my way into God's good graces. Instead, it is God's rewiring of our appetites—what the Puritans called "affections." The way God sees things, if we want to change our behavior, we need to get to our appetites, and the only One who can get to our hearts is God. God's first act of love is to change our hearts, giving us the capacity to both love him and experience his performance-free love for us. But God is also interested in our hearts, because if he can change them, he'll get our actions. What we do flows from who we are.

Parenting young kids can be wearisome, especially when they are toddlers. Searching for answers and rest, Korie and I found Ted Tripp's *Shepherding a Child's Heart*. He spends a lot of time talking about law-based parenting, an approach to raising kids that stops at behaviors. You know, the things we parents bark to our children: "Sit down." "Eat your food." "Take the dice out of your mouth." (Yes, we did have a child who enjoyed chewing dice.) As our kids grow older, this external-based parenting continues, but just with different commands: "Stop texting at dinner." "Read your Bible." "Pray." "Don't visit certain websites." Ted Tripp isn't against having behavioral standards for our kids; he just pushes us to go further as parents. Instead of remaining in the land of *what* (behaviors), he suggests venturing beyond to the *why* (our hearts). "Why don't you want to spend time with God?" "Why wouldn't you want to share a part of your allowance with the poor?" "Why are you so devastated when you lose that you throw a fit?" These questions force us to look at our hearts.

Why is it important that we get to the heart? Because our hearts feed our behaviors. True righteousness of the solid-gold variety—a righteousness that is both internal and external and surpasses that of the religious leaders—only happens when we have redeemed hearts and hands. So if we want to change, it's not a matter of trying harder but of desiring more.

But it's here that things get a little messy. We are as impotent to change our hearts as a person is to perform bypass surgery on themselves. If God doesn't get to our hearts, our hands (behaviors) will not know the joys of lasting change.

The television show *Hoarders* chronicles people who can't seem to get rid of their stuff. I've seen episodes in which a small house is packed with nearly a half million books, and with kitchens so long neglected that when they were finally cleaned, dead animals were discovered.

In each show, help comes with a knock on the door. Typically, a few people show up with the task of decluttering the home, but there's usually also a psychologist. The message is obvious: It makes no sense to clean the house without taking a peek underneath the hood and into the heart of the owner. In order for their behavior to change, their internal disorder must be addressed and healthy desires must be nurtured.

Writing to the Philippians, Paul weds our hands and hearts: "Therefore, my dear friends, as you have always obeyed—not only in my presence, but now much more in my absence—continue to work out your salvation with fear and trembling, for it is God who works in you to will and to act in order to fulfill his good purpose" (Philippians 2:12–13).

God cares about our actions. He wants us to give to the poor, love our enemies, and engage in peacemaking. Christ followers should pray and read their Bibles. But these good deeds will not last long unless they are fueled by new-covenant hearts. "It is God who works in you to will and to act in order to fulfill his good purpose." The path from greed to generosity, from sinfulness to holiness, begins with desire, and righteous desire can only come from God.

King David understood this. Frustrated over his sin, he didn't just will himself to do better; instead, he prayed to God, "Create in me a pure heart, O God, and renew a steadfast spirit within me" (Psalm 51:10). David knew what Jesus preached and Paul wrote: The path to change, to becoming impossibly good, begins with a new heart.

In his sermon, Jesus lays on us an impossible standard in order to deflate our aspirations for man-made goodness, while at the same time thrusting us into the arms of the only One who can make us good—God. The Sermon on the Mount is impossibly possible. We have no hope of living this kingdom ethic on our own, but there is One who gives us the power to exceed the righteousness of the Pharisees and the teachers of the law. When both our actions and affections are touched by God's grace, we surpass these religious leaders.

anamorphic pride

WHEN GOOD BECOMES BAD

The essential vice, the utmost evil, is Pride.
C. S. Lewis, *Mere Christianity*

As a teen, Shannon Mall was my playground. I spent a lot of hours there, laughing with friends, working up the courage to talk to girls, and then, at some point—faking like I had to go to the bathroom—stealing a few moments in the art gallery. I figured it wasn't cool for a fifteen-year-old to tell his girl-crazed buddies he was leaving to peruse the art gallery, but I was smitten. The paintings in this gallery were called "anamorphic art," where an artist inserts an object beneath the surface that can only be detected if you look long enough from a certain angle. Sometimes I'd see the hidden object immediately, but then there were occasions when I just knew it wasn't there. Asking one of the workers for help, they would smile and tell me to look closer. Sure enough, after a few more moments, I would see the object. I just had to look more closely.

In a well-quoted passage in his masterpiece *Mere Christianity*, C. S. Lewis compares our lives to anamorphic paintings, where pride is the inserted object that lurks well below the surface of all sin:

There is one vice of which no man in the world is free; which every one in the world loathes when he sees it in someone else . . . The vice I am talking of is Pride or Self-Conceit . . . According to Christian teachers, the essential vice, the utmost evil, is Pride. Unchastity, anger, greed, drunkenness, and all that, are mere fleabites in comparison: it was through Pride that the devil became the devil: Pride leads to every other vice: it is the complete anti-God state of mind.[1]

When I first encountered these words, I had to reread them, mulling them over slowly, wondering if they were true. I thought back to those moments just after I had finished preaching, when I had lied to an eager congregant who wanted to know if I had read their email. "Sure," I responded with little thought. "No, you didn't," the Holy Spirit said, pointing out my untruth. But why did I lie? Well, I needed this person to think I am a great pastor, and everyone knows all great pastors read every email. I didn't lie just for the sake of being dishonest; I lied to ensure they would continue to think well of me. Why did I lie? Pride.

Or take the timid person. What if I told you that timidity is a face of pride? It is. So a person in your life offends you—I mean really wrongs you. Everything within you says you should say something, but you don't. Why? Well, you could be worried that a truth encounter in which you challenge them will mean they'll no longer like, well, *you*. So *you* stay away from the hard conversations and feign as if everything is all right—not to protect the other person or the relationship but really to protect *you*. See the pride?

Someone once described prayer as the soul's dependence on God. The act of prayer is akin to a fatigued three-year-old raising her hands, saying, "Daddy, can you carry me?" It takes a lot of humility to pray. If this is true, then every day I spend in prayerlessness is a day wasted in pride—a day in which I say to God, "I got this." Prayer can become like those oxygen masks on airplanes—something to be used only in case of emergency. See the pride?

C. S. Lewis is right. The essential vice is pride. The common denominator in all sin is pride. More than analyzing the human condition, Lewis's diagnosis helps us unpack Jesus' teachings in the Sermon on the Mount. As we travel deeper into the sermon, we are going to learn more about the problem of man-made goodness that deters us from experiencing the indestructible life.

A BAD KIND OF GOOD

We've been chatting about God's mind-blowing, performance-free love, a kind of love we all want in which we have a future hope and a transcendent purpose. Everyone wants a life like this. We just tend to get turned around on our way there. Confused, we journey the path that billions have taken for centuries, namely, moralism. Do enough good things, and you'll arrive. Be true to yourself and don't harm others, and the meaning, value, and significance are at your fingertips—or so we think. Sounds good; it's just at odds with what Jesus teaches in the gospel of Matthew and especially in the Sermon on the Mount.

In Matthew 5–7, Jesus lays on us an ethical impossibility. We have to surpass the Pharisees and the teachers of the law in the goodness department. As we saw in the last chapter, the only way this happens is if we give ourselves completely to the grace and mercy of the only One who can make us good—God. At the moment of salvation, God gives us a new heart, transforming our behaviors so our righteousness is no longer just outward, but internal as well. This solid-gold, God-worked goodness beats the gold-plated "goodness" of the religious leaders any day.

Taking a few more steps deeper into the sermon, Jesus points out in Matthew 6 that man-made goodness is a contradiction of terms—an oxymoron. There really is no such thing as man-made goodness. Good, Jesus preaches, is actually bad; morality is immoral if its source is not God.

As Jesus begins his message, his attention is not on the masses but on his handpicked followers—his disciples. Now in chapter 6, he decides to give some human illustrations:

> "Be careful not to practice your righteousness in front of others to be seen by them. If you do, you will have no reward from your Father in heaven.
> "So when you give to the needy, do not announce it with trumpets, as the hypocrites do in the synagogues and on the streets, to be honored by others. Truly I tell you, they have received their reward in full."
>
> *Matthew 6:1–2*

In pretty blunt language, Jesus calls out the Pharisees and the teachers of the law, referring to them as hypocrites. To be fair, Jesus does affirm that these religious leaders do good things. If you read the rest of chapter 6, you will see they not only gave to the needy but also fasted and prayed. What's more, Jesus assumes that his followers will do the same: "So *when* you give to the needy . . ." (emphasis mine). The question is not if, but when. The way of Jesus is not just about new motives and desires; it's also seen in fruitful actions that benefit others.

You don't need a seminary degree to discern that Jesus is not waving pom-poms and cheering on the efforts of the religious leaders. Quite the opposite. Jesus wants us to steer clear of these philanthropic, praying, and ascetic leaders. Stay away from those who are doing good? Huh?

Jesus is disturbed not by the what of the religious leaders but by their why. They gave, fasted, and prayed "to be honored by others." And in words that would make anyone flinch in discomfort, Jesus calls them "hypocrites."

Matthew is writing in Greek, and the Greek word for *hypocrite* means "actor." An actor is a person who pretends. They embody a given character and interpret that person's life onstage in the hopes that the audience will take to their performance. Any actor will tell you who they are on the stage is often miles apart from who they are off the stage.

The fact that Jesus would use this theatrical term to describe philanthropic, prayerful, fasting religious leaders stings. The old adage is true: Never judge a book by its cover—or in this case, a person by his performance. A lot of people appear to do good things, but there's plenty of distance between who they are in the spotlight and who they are offstage.

I spent the summer after my freshman year in Bible college interning at a small church in the Midwest. The senior pastor and his wife showed me great kindness by allowing me to live with them. During the next several months, I must have asked scores of questions, trying to glean all the wisdom I could from this godly pastor. We spent Saturday mornings fishing, where my questions continued. Standing in the back of a hospital room, I watched him pray for the hurting. On many weeknights, I would rap gently on the door to his home study because I wanted to see how he prepared his sermon. I adored him. He was my hero.

So you can sympathize with my sadness when my father called me a few months into the next semester to tell me this pastor had been removed from his church. A woman in the congregation had confessed to carrying on an affair with him. Over time, more women came forward. When offered an opportunity to confess and go through a process of restoration, he bristled. My one-time hero ended up divorcing his wife, and now several decades later, he continues in his own dark night of the soul. I can't help it, but when I read Matthew 6 and see a word like *hypocrite*, I see his face.

Hypocrite is a very strong word, so we need to tread lightly. In a sense, all sin is hypocrisy, and who among us fully live up to our ideals? Anyone? I'd like to believe I don't wear rose-colored glasses when it comes to the church, but I really do think it's unfair to single out the church as if she is the only repository for hypocrites. When the fraternity Sigma Alpha Epsilon came under fire because of the racism of a few in its University of Oklahoma chapter, I'm sure many of its members pleaded with the onlookers not to judge the whole by the racist hypocrisy of a few. Every institution has its hypocrites. No one bats a thousand in the authentic category.

What Jesus is getting at is not the momentary breaches in integrity called sin. Instead, he's calling to light those who appear to be public successes but are really private failures. The hypocrite of Matthew 6 is the person who works so hard at perception but labors little at character. It's the hypocrite who wants to be adored for who you think she is, not for who she actually is. And the materials used by the hypocrites of Matthew 6 to construct their perception are the hammers and nails of good works. Morality, Jesus implies, becomes immorality when it is done for the applause of man and not for the glory of God.

I can't stand in condemnation over my fallen Midwest hero. Over the years, I've counseled marriages while at times treating my wife like dirt. I've exhorted others to read their Bibles and pray while going through long stretches of prayerlessness. And I have pleaded with people to live holy lives while indulging seasons of carnality.

Jesus' words in the opening verses of Matthew 6 are hard to hear: Moralism stinks. Good for the sake of good or to be seen by others or to feel better about yourself is bad. Doing good even solely for the benefit of others reeks. If you continue to eavesdrop on Jesus' conversation with his disciples, you'll hear him say, "When you give to the needy, do not let your left hand know what your right hand is doing, so that your giving may be in secret. Then your Father, who sees what is done in secret, will reward you" (Matthew 6:3–4).

Do good, Jesus says. Just make sure the aim of your goodness isn't horizontal, but rather vertical. The Bible knows of only one kind of good—one that results in the glory of God, not in the applause of man.

THE OTHER

When I started a multiethnic church some years ago, we began to attract a lot of young people who—how should I say this— the world would label as "liberals." Many were whites who were repulsed by their wealthy parents' lifestyle choices, so they moved into the hood and lived as a minority. I found them to be the first to sign up to build a home or feed the poor. As we grew, our church began to gain a reputation of being the only church doing it right. If you were really serious about the poor and about ethnic diversity, then Fellowship Memphis was where you needed to be—or so they said. Over time, I didn't like what I smelled.

I soon realized our congregation was basing its self-esteem on the perceived failures and shortcomings of other people and churches. C. S. Lewis observed that each person's pride can't exist without competing with others.[2] Pride can only be built on the supposed "inferiorities" of others—in comparing ourselves to others and in taking pleasure, not "out of having something, only out of having more of it than the next man."[3] If there was no public school, where would the pride be in sending my child to a private one? If every house in every zip code was the exact same, where's the pride when I pull into my garage? If there was only one ethnicity, the insidious pride of racism would be extinct. In order for pride to metastasize, it must feed off the other

The sexually pure need the promiscuous; the generous need the greedy; and established churches that rent need ones that go into debt to purchase a building to give them a sense of inflated identity. But if my identity is located in my morality and not in Christ, then I join the acting troop of hypocrites Jesus calls out in Matthew 6.

Moments after notifying me of my Midwest pastor's removal, Dad asked if I had noticed anything weird with him. I offered a quick no, while my mind scanned the events of the previous summer. "Well, Dad, something did seem a bit strange," I confessed.

An attractive woman about my age, who had grown up in that church and gone off to college, came home pregnant out of wedlock. She was mired in a shame as visible as her third-trimester stomach, and the women of the church rallied to her support. Word soon spread of a baby shower to be held in her honor. When our pastor received the news, he was incensed. On a Sunday morning, he preached an impromptu sermon on the evils of fornication, while the pregnant college dropout dabbed her eyes. There would be no baby shower; "to do so would be an endorsement of her sin," he reasoned. I didn't agree, but I had found his "righteous indignation" and "conviction" admirable.

Now I'm being told that the same man of conviction was cheating on his wife in hotel rooms across the city while preaching extemporaneous Sunday sermons on the evils of sexual immorality. It's one thing to sin, but to use the failures of others as a stage to stand on, saying, "Look at me," is nauseating. The problem with pride is that it magnifies the faults of others while being blinded to one's own. Pride is like looking at your reflection in one of those distorted mirrors that make you look a lot bigger than what you actually are. Travel the road of man-made goodness, and this is where we will end up every time.

In Joe DiMaggio's first game back with the Yankees after serving in World War II, he decided to walk onto the field moments before the game, tip his cap, and show appreciation to the tens of thousands who had filled Yankee Stadium to celebrate their beloved center fielder's return. Picking up his young son, Joe DiMaggio Jr., he walked out on the field as the crowd began to chant, "Joe! Joe! Joe!" Wearing a huge smile, Joe Jr. looked at his father and exclaimed, "Dad, they're calling my name!"

This is pride—spiritual plagiarism in which we take credit for God's work without citing our source. And while this story may seem cute, pride isn't. It's what got Satan evicted from heaven and the first family removed from the garden. Pride led to Israel's exile and nailed Jesus to a cross. Man-made morality is no laughing matter. Unchecked, it will not only keep us from experiencing God's performance-free love, but it could have devastating repercussions for the life to come.

# of hawks and doves

THE TRANSFORMATION OF REPENTANCE

"Not everyone who says to me, 'Lord, Lord,'
will enter the kingdom of heaven."
Jesus, in Matthew 7:21

Weddings and funerals make for great blooper material—that is, if you're the minister and not the bride or the family of the deceased. I will never forget the last funeral I did while serving as a young minister at a church in California. A young man named Andrew had died, and his grandmother asked if I would do the eulogy. Both devastated and honored, I agreed, rehearsed my sermon, grabbed my vestments, and made my way to the church, which sat on a busy thoroughfare a couple hundred yards from the Rose Bowl Stadium.

When I walked into the pastor's study, I knew this was going to be interesting. Looking me up and down, this elderly pastor began barking instructions at me as if I was some army recruit on my first day at boot camp. I was to do the eulogy (which I already knew) and then the "releasing of the dulves" ceremony. Now, I had no clue what a "releasing of the dulves" ceremony was, but because he was treating me like some rookie, I wasn't going to ask. I just started asking questions, trying to get him to talk more about these "dulves"—and finally I understood he was really trying to say "dove," but it came out "dulve." But even though I had clarity on his words, I had no clue about the ceremony. I had never done one of these dove things before, but there was no way *he* was going to know that.

So I preached the eulogy, and then the four hundred or so people who had packed the little church to pay their respects to Andrew ventured outside, where I began my extemporaneous explanation on the dove about to be released. "This dove represents Andrew's spirit," I said. Then remembering Paul's words, I continued: "To be absent from the body is to be present with the Lord." *That's good*, I thought, while I ventured on: "And when we release this dove, it will fly up into the sky, just like Andrew's spirit has gone to be with Jesus." For my first shot at this "dulve" thing, I'm feeling really good about myself. Rookie that, veteran pastor!

I nodded at the man who was in charge of the dove to let him know I was ready. He reached down into a brown paper bag with the word *DOVE* written on it in large crayon font. Some thoughtful person had even poked two holes into the bag so the dove could breathe. Gently, this man held the dove in his hands and let it go, where it fluttered just above our ducking heads. Moments later, a hawk that had been eyeing this whole "dulve ceremony" jumped on its back and ate it, leaving a trail of feathers. There was a collective gasp, followed by an onslaught of questions all pointed my way. *What did this say about Andrew? Was this some omen? Is he really in hell?* I had no answers. I muttered some words, offered a quick prayer, and left. This would make for great reality TV.

IT'S COMPLICATED

Their questions were good ones. Honest ones. Just moments before, we all felt certain Andrew was in heaven, but post-hawk, we started to wonder where Andrew was now. *Was there something in Andrew's life we didn't know about? Was this just some coincidence, or a sign of some sort?* I'm really confused by it all, to be honest.

Sometimes I find myself confused over my own life. *Where am I headed? Am I really going to heaven?* Dr. Martin Luther King Jr. wrestled with similar questions. He once said in a sermon that each of us has two selves—a higher and lower self. Sociologist Michael Eric Dyson believes Dr. King was giving us a peek into his own well-known struggles and confessing to his now all-too-familiar complexities. Maybe Dr. King was admitting something we all know too well. Some days, we seem to be doves, and other days hawks. Good and evil lock arms in a daily contest in our lives. If we were to put a Facebook status update on our souls, it would say, "It's complicated."

As Jesus finishes his Sermon on the Mount, he wades into the confusion we feel about our souls. Look at Matthew 7:21–23:

> "Not everyone who says to me, 'Lord, Lord,' will enter the kingdom of heaven, but only the one who does the will of my Father who is in heaven. Many will say to me on that day, 'Lord, Lord, did we not prophesy in your name and in your name drive out demons and in your name perform many miracles?' Then I will tell them plainly, 'I never knew you. Away from me, you evildoers!'"

You don't have to have the gift of discernment to figure out who Jesus is talking about here. It's the Pharisees, the same group of people he cautioned his disciples not to mimic in chapter 6. Think about what Jesus is saying. He points to a group of people who say the right things by calling him Lord. They even seem to do the right things—like prophesy, drive out demons, and do "many miracles," all while invoking the name of Jesus.

But when everything is said and done, Jesus says he never knew them. Talk about complicated!

If I read this right, hell will have some parking spaces reserved for people who went to seminary, pastored churches, had thriving itinerant ministries, sang in the choir, and served on deacon or elder boards. I mean, if I really understand what Jesus is saying, hell will have incredibly moral people—dutiful fathers who never abandoned their kids or cheated on their wives. Jesus isn't talking about the woman leaving the bar in the middle of the night with some dude she just met or about a group of drug addicts. He is addressing money-giving, synagogue-attending, Scripture-memorizing, law-abiding, so-called good people he says he never knew. Looks can be deceiving. Man-made morality independent of a relationship with Jesus is not good enough to barge one's way into heaven.

Growing up in Atlanta, I had a friend named Anthony. He was an amazing basketball player who announced to us one day that he was going to try out for the Georgia Tech basketball team. Every day he went to tryouts. He wowed the coaches with his speed and agility. His ability to handle the ball, drive to the hole, and shoot a long-range jump shot impressed the head coach so much that at the end of tryouts, he told Anthony he was on the team. We were awed that Anthony pulled it off.

A few days later, however, the coach told Anthony what we already knew: As great a basketball player as he was, he couldn't be on the team any longer. Anthony had never enrolled in school! He was not—nor did he have any plans to be—a student. For several weeks, Anthony ran sprints, participated in drills, and did what the other players did in the same place they did it in. He was dressed like a Georgia Tech Yellow Jacket, but he ended up having to leave the team, because while he looked like a Yellow Jacket, did what Yellow Jackets did, and moved about in the same venue that Yellow Jackets moved about in, he had no relationship with the school, and the jig was up.

If I read Jesus right in Matthew 7, the same will be said for a lot of people who think they are Christians but in reality are not. This is a really hard word. Jesus says it's quite possible to look like a Christian, hang out in the same venues (church), and even engage in the same activities (giving, praying, preaching, etc.), and not be an actual Christian. It really *is* complicated.

Jesus' words should shock us. I find them to be some of the most unsettling in the Scriptures. And the reason his words are so unsettling is that they do violence to the notion that I can claim to have experienced God's performance-free love without having my life change one bit. What Jesus says here compels me to turn introspective, asking, "Am I a hawk or a dove?" It's a question I'm constantly mulling over in my mind: *Am I genuinely saved? Have I truly encountered the Indestructible One?* The apostle Paul would say these questions are not only good ones but also necessary ones. In his first letter to the Corinthians, Paul writes, "Everyone ought to examine themselves" (1 Corinthians 11:28). Then in his second letter, he writes, "Examine yourselves to see whether you are in the faith; test yourselves" (2 Corinthians 13:5). Yes, Jesus wants us to be sure of our salvation, but as a jeweler scrutinizes a diamond before he gives the certificate of authenticity, so we should look inward into the deep places of our souls and entrust ourselves to the mercy of God to continue his work.

THERE IS NO THIRD WAY IN THE WAY OF JESUS

If you listen closely enough to Jesus' words in Matthew 7, you will find yourself conflicted over a paradox. On the one hand, Jesus muddies the water by saying, in effect, "Wait a minute.

Don't be so quick to assume certain people are basking in God's performance-free love, just because they say so or because of outward appearances. It's complicated." On the other hand, both before and after his words about true and false disciples in Matthew 7, he gives rich analogies of two gates, two trees, and two foundations. Jesus says that when it comes to life in the kingdom, there are only two options—in or out. It's as if Jesus is saying, "It's really simple."

Jesus begins by pointing out two gates—a broad one and a narrow one. If I close my eyes, I don't see a fire-and-brimstone Jesus happily condemning people to hell. Instead, I see a pleading Jesus begging us to "enter through the narrow gate. For wide is the gate and broad is the road that leads to destruction, and many enter through it" (Matthew 7:13). Next, Jesus says there are really only two kinds of trees—healthy and diseased. "By their fruit," Jesus says, "you will recognize them" (verse 16). Finally, the whole chapter ends with Jesus pointing out two homes. Both encounter storms. One is left standing, while the other collapses. The difference? The foundation. Generally speaking, Jesus says, there are only two kinds of foundations— good and bad. In fact, all of Matthew 7 can be summed up in one word: *two*. Not three, not seven, not twenty-seven. Two.

God's offer of a performance-free love is not just one option among a buffet of many. If I understand Jesus, it's an all-or-nothing proposition. Either I am walking through the narrow gate or I am on the broad path with a reservation for eternal separation from God.

If I seem blunt, it's because I feel deeply that our Christian culture has tried to create and pitch a third alternative, which has wreaked havoc in the church and has grave eternal consequences. This third way pretty much says, "Do whatever makes you happy, show up to church, say a few prayers, read the Bible occasionally, and Jesus will help you pull off 'Project You.' Add just enough Jesus to your life to make you acceptable, but not too much to make you fanatical." This is third-way theology.

In one of my former churches, I was asked by an attender if I would bless the home he and his significant other had just moved into. I didn't think he was married, but for clarity's sake, I asked, and he confirmed they were not married. "So let me get this straight," I said as gently as possible. "You want me to pray God's blessing over your home and the very bed where you and your girlfriend will knowingly violate God's ideal for your relationship?" He was angry with me for what he considered to be my narrow-mindedness. The problem isn't so much what they were doing, but the fact that they were pursuing this way of life while claiming to be followers of Jesus. Their rationale went something like this: (1) This makes us happy; (2) of course, God wants us to be happy; (3) so, pastor, come and bless this. Moralistic Therapeutic Deism is third-way theology—the very thing Jesus speaks against in the heart of his sermon.

Third-way theology doesn't lament over sin. Third-way theology makes room for the extramarital affair while still attending church. Third-way theology glosses over greed, excuses sin, and calls holiness legalism. Where the church has sought to widen the narrow gate, her light has dimmed and the salt has become saltless.

I want to plead with us the way Jesus does. No, Jesus is not arguing for perfection here. Can we take a moment and remember who he is talking to? His disciples. Peter would disown him three times. The rest, except for John, would abandon him at the cross. Over and over, they were chided for their lack of faith and their prideful, petulant arguing. The disciples were deeply flawed people, yet all but Judas ventured through the narrow gate, blemishes and all. This encourages me. I'm in daily need of fresh grace. My pride shames me. There have been seasons when I have indulged the flesh. Something tells me you can relate. Praise God that "his compassions never fail. They are new every morning; great is [his] faithfulness" (Lamentations 3:22–23).

A lot of Christ followers idolize the first-century church, longing for the church of today to be like the church of AD 50-something. Not so fast. Have you read the book of 1 Corinthians, which tells of a man who was sleeping with his stepmother? The Corinthians were so immature that they sued one another in court instead of working out their problems within the church. And if that wasn't enough, Paul had to talk extensively to them about the rampant sexual immorality of several members who were soliciting prostitutes. So much for wanting to be like the first-century church!

But through it all, Paul refers to the Corinthians as brothers and sisters. In chapter 3, he chalks up their sin to spiritual immaturity, calling them "mere infants" (verse 1). Yes, Paul implies, it is possible to be a follower of Jesus Christ and indulge in seasons of sin. So are Jesus and Paul at odds? No. How do we get to the bottom of this?

Everyone sins. Those who aren't in relationship with Jesus do, just like those of us who are walking in God's performance-free love. The difference is summed up in a word called *repentance*. Look at what Paul says to the Corinthians: "Yet now I am happy, not because you were made sorry, but because your sorrow led you to repentance . . . Godly sorrow brings repentance that leads to salvation and leaves no regret" (2 Corinthians 7:9–10).

Paul gives two indicator lights I have found helpful when I wonder in seasons of doubt if I am really living in performance-free love. First, do I grieve over my sin? Does it bring me sorrow? Everyone sins; however, followers of Jesus Christ are *disturbed* by their sin. But sorrow is not enough. So Paul adds that godly sorrow should lead to repentance. To repent means to change our direction. Repentance is a progressive distancing between myself and sin, wonderfully brought about by the kindness of God (Romans 2:4). Every follower of Jesus Christ should be able to look through the rearview mirror of their journey with him and conclude two things: First, I have not made it all the way to where I should be. But second, I am not where I once was. Jesus is changing me. I am repenting. As I heard one pastor say, "When I first got saved, I cussed at the drop of a hat. Now since following Jesus, I don't cuss that fast anymore." While his words garnered a lot of laughs, they were laced with rich biblical truth. He's admitting to sin, but he's also seeing a change. He hasn't arrived, but he sees the fruit of repentance.

THE FRUIT OF FAILURE

If Jesus seems unduly harsh toward these moral religious leaders in Matthew 7, it's because a few chapters earlier, his cousin John invited them to examine themselves and reveal the genuineness of their salvation. "Produce fruit," John said, "in keeping with repentance" (Matthew 3:8). Now in chapter 7, Jesus says, "Thus, by their fruit you will recognize them" (verse 20). Fruit is evidence. How do you know it's an orange tree? Well, you see oranges. How do you know you're in relationship with Jesus, living in God's performance-free love? You see fruit—and one such fruit is repentance.

Do you not see the beautiful irony here? Repentance happens when there is godly sorrow, but for there to be godly sorrow, there must be sin. This warms my heart. I am certainly not encouraging sin or promoting a cavalier attitude toward our sin. Instead, Paul's words of grief and repentance about sin challenge us to view our failures not as a barrier but as an opportunity.

Sin doesn't disqualify me from serving God; it opens wide the doors for sorrow and repentance to flood in—evidences I'm being washed daily in the ocean of God's performance-free love.

It's ironic but true. The only way we really know growth is through failure. One of the strongest evidences of our authentic faith is seen in how we navigate our sin. This is a truth the writer of Proverbs alluded to when he wrote, "For though the righteous fall seven times, they rise again" (Proverbs 24:16). This verse blesses me because in describing the person who fails multiple times, the Bible calls him or her righteous. Why? Through their sin, they get up. They repent.

This is the story of King David, the second king of Israel. Having committed adultery and murder, he got up by repenting of his sin, and when it's all said and done, he is known as the man after God's own heart.

This is also the story of Bill McCartney, former head football coach of the Colorado Buffaloes and the founder of Promise Keepers. In the early days of his marriage, he was an alcoholic and even had a one-night stand with another woman. Consumed by grief, he immersed himself in God's performance-free love, leaned on God's grace, and repented. I've had the honor of meeting and being around Coach Mac, and I can tell you I haven't met a more tender, sweet, grace-filled, godly man. He truly embodies Proverbs 24:16: "Though the righteous fall seven times, they rise again."

Frustrated and weary over your sin? Wondering if you are a genuine child of God? Concerned about whether you're walking through the narrow gate or whether you're a diseased tree or a house built with a shoddy foundation moments from disaster? Two questions will solve it all: Does your sin bring you sorrow? Does that sorrow turn into repentance—a change in direction?

authentic goodness

the good solution

FROM PERFORMING TO ABIDING

*"Come to me, all you who are weary and
burdened, and I will give you rest."*
Jesus, in Matthew 11:28

The euphoria a person feels when they first take drugs is unlike anything they've ever experienced. Many spend a significant part of their lives chasing that first high. They will empty bank accounts, steal from family members, and put their lives on the line to replicate the "joy" that was theirs the first moment drugs entered their system. But it's all for nothing. They may catch flashes of joy, but for the most part, they only know sorrow, despair, and shame.

I've never tried narcotics, but I do know the emptiness that comes with trying to find joy and self-worth in good deeds. I know the ecstasy of generosity and the temporary high of saying no to temptation. But these highs are short-lived. I sin often. Given to unholy thoughts, consistent pride, and other sins, I know too well the shame of the drug addict. So when I crash, there had better be something to hold on to other than white-knuckled morality.

The desire to matter is a part of being human. When people no longer feel or want this, they can become destructive to others and themselves. Our persistent grasping for true meaning, value, and significance takes us down many paths—one of the most prevalent being moralism. Many of us try to perform, believing that if at the end of our lives the "good works" side of the scale is heavier than the bad side, God will be pleased with us and heaven will be within reach. This line of thinking has been bought into by both the irreligious and religious. Sure, Christians know better than to put it in these terms, but our pharisaical self-righteousness and judgmental spirits say otherwise. Maybe you don't condemn others, but only yourself. You wonder if God still loves you, even as you wallow in self-hatred and doubt over past and present failures. We have been hardwired to think that God wants our performance.

In the Sermon on the Mount, Jesus takes a sledgehammer to self-righteous morality and decimates any thought we may have about tap-dancing our way into God's good graces. The last several chapters of this book should have left us feeling a little overwhelmed as we examined the impossible standard Jesus lays on us in his sermon. As Jesus finishes his sermon, we should be like the sinner in the temple who beat his breast, begging for mercy (Luke 18:13). God help us all.

But what is the way forward? Do we stop writing checks or saying no to sin? Do we no longer need to read our Bibles or pray? No, these things are still good; they just need to be seen in a different light. God's performance-free love leaves plenty of room for good deeds as a response to his love, *not* an "in order to." While these good deeds are never primary, what is primary is an abiding relationship with Jesus. This is the punch line to Jesus' message in Matthew 11.

COME

If you've spent some time in church, you are probably familiar with Matthew 11:28: "Come to me, all you who are weary and burdened, and I will give you rest." It's hard to imagine the same One who had some pretty tough things to say a few chapters earlier in the Sermon on the Mount now standing tenderly with open arms, inviting the weary and worn-out to rest in him.

But who exactly are the weary? Over the years, I've heard this passage preached many times. Each time, the point has been that if you're worn-out by sickness, a wayward child, a bad marriage, or a season of unemployment, you just need to come to Jesus. Now while I think these are great secondary applications, this is not the primary meaning of Jesus' invitation. Jesus is not speaking in general to those who are beaten down by life. No, he has a very specific audience in mind.

Let's take a few moments to try to wrap our arms around Jesus' words. As Matthew 11 begins, Jesus' relative John has landed in jail. He must have been there for a considerable length of time, because John commissions his followers to ask if Jesus is the one (verse 3). You know what John is really getting at, don't you? If Jesus is the one—the Messiah—then John wants to know why he's taking so long to get him out of jail. *It's not rocket science*, John has to be thinking. *Say a prayer. Clap your hands. Utter some words, and I'm out of here.* In response to John's request, Jesus sends a cryptic message to his relative—a quotation from Isaiah 61:1. Being steeped in the Word, John knew this familiar text: "The Spirit of the Sovereign LORD is on me, because the LORD has anointed me to proclaim good news to the poor. He has sent me to bind up the brokenhearted, to proclaim freedom for the captives and release from darkness for the prisoners." In Matthew's gospel, Jesus quotes from Isaiah 61:1 but leaves out a crucial part: "Go back and report to John what you hear and see: The blind receive sight, the lame walk, those who have leprosy are cleansed, the deaf hear, the dead are raised, and the good news is proclaimed to the poor. Blessed is anyone who does not stumble on account of me" (Matthew 11:4–6). Did you catch what part of Isaiah 61:1 Jesus omits? That's right. The part about captives being set free and prisoners being released from darkness.

Jesus knows John will be disappointed by the news because he ends by asking his relative to not be offended by him. In essence, Jesus says, *John, I am the one—and no, you're not going to get out of jail.* True to Jesus' words, John stays incarcerated, dies, and has his head delivered on a platter to Herod's wife and stepdaughter (Matthew 14:10–12).

If I can just pause and come to your neighborhood, Jesus' words may rub us the wrong way, but it's a truth worth grappling with in a world that thinks Jesus exists to make us happy: He is God, regardless of how our circumstances pan out. He's worthy to be praised when breast cancer is cured—and just as worthy when the disease takes a life. We don't follow God for outcomes or for the benefits package; we follow him because we love him.

"Blessed is anyone who does not stumble on account of me."

With John's disciples on their way back, Jesus now turns to the crowd and preaches the eulogy of his relative. Remember, this is Jesus' relative he is talking about, so what lies ahead is very likely filled with emotion, even some tears. He begins by reflecting on John's ministry. John was known as "the Baptist" because of his frequent baptisms. Whom did he baptize? Jews. That's right, John baptized synagogue-attending, Scripture-memorizing, generous-giving Jews. But John did more than baptize; he preached, calling people to repent—to turn from their sins. How effective was John's call to repentance? Jesus answers in Matthew 11:16–17: "To what can I compare this generation? They are like children sitting in the marketplaces and calling out to others: 'We played the pipe for you, and you did not dance; we sang a dirge, and you did not mourn.'" This is a powerful image. In Jesus' day, pipes were played at festive occasions like weddings. When you heard them, you knew it was your cue to dance. A dirge was played at a funeral. Like Pavlov's dog, when you heard the dirge, you were supposed to mourn. But in Matthew 11, Jesus compares John's ministry to a pipe being played and no one dancing, a dirge being sung and no one mourning. John did his part (playing the pipe and singing the dirge); the people just didn't dance or mourn—they didn't repent. Jesus' illustration is not an indictment on John's ministry. Instead, it is a gut-wrenching critique of these so-called good, moral people. Whom does Jesus address in Matthew 11? Moral people who see nothing wrong with their lives and who refuse to repent and turn to their only hope of being good— Jesus Christ.

The eulogy isn't over. Beginning in verse 20, Jesus turns his attention to several cities—Chorazin, Bethsaida, and Capernaum. These three cities—the buckle of the ancient Bible Belt—were filled with religious people trying their best to be upright and moral. Jesus had visited these cities and had done many mighty works there. These people *saw* the lame walk, withered hands restored, and demons driven out. What was the result? Jesus says they did not repent. Here they were—witnesses to miracles performed by Jesus, yet unmoved in their own feeble attempts at morality. When the miracles were over, their lives remained the same.

I'm not here to pick on the charismatic movement. I affirm all the gifts and have served in churches considered to be charismatic. But Jesus' words to these religious cities should be carefully read by all, especially my charismatic friends. Jesus is saying that spiritual gifts—even sign gifts—aren't enough to save people. There must be more.

I'll never forget the time Korie and I went with friends to an upscale steak house. We ordered our steaks, and a few moments later, I was served sorbet. Young and naive, I wondered aloud why they were bringing dessert before the main course. Korie kicked me pretty hard and whispered that the sorbet was to cleanse the palate and ready me for the steak. I felt pretty silly.

The more I think about it and study the Scriptures, that's how it is with the sign gifts like miracles and healing. These gifts (among others) cleanse the soul's palate, making people ready to hear and receive the gospel. Sign gifts are the sorbet, but the cross is the main course. Read the book of Acts. There's always a missional component to the sign gifts. What prepared the crowd in Acts 2 for the main course of the cross was the sorbet of tongues. Miracles may change your circumstances, but they can't transform your soul. Only the cross can do that.

When we arrive at Jesus' words in Matthew 11:28, there's no doubt whom he has been talking to. Jesus has been addressing weary, worn-out people who have spent their lives on the treadmill of moralism and see no end in sight. They have been relentless in their pursuit of good works, even to the point of becoming baptized and seeing mighty works performed, but have noticed little change. These are the weary folks Jesus invites to come to him, not just people going through difficult times in their lives.

The treadmill of morality is wearisome. At what point do you ever check the box and think you've finally done enough? How many church services does it take to forever feel good about yourself? What's the dollar amount you can donate to charity for your conscience to be permanently soothed? And how many times do you need to share your faith to be convinced you're an eternally good person filled with meaning and value?

Whenever Jehovah's Witnesses come to our home, I try to

point this out. Usually two of them knock on our door, and being a touch mischievous, I like to pick on the trainee.

> **Me:** So why are you knocking on doors on a Saturday morning?
>
> **Trainee:** We're just trying to tell people about our faith and get into the 144,000 the book of Revelation talks about.
>
> **Me:** Really? So how many doors do you have to knock on to make it in?
>
> **Trainee:** Not sure. (Looks to trainer for help.)
>
> **Me:** And who's managing this list of 144,000?
>
> **Trainee:** Not sure. (Looks again to trainer.)
>
> **Me:** So at what point do you know you've done enough to make it in?
>
> *I never really get a good answer.*

Please don't mistake me for being some evangelistic bully. These same questions with slight variations can be asked to Christians:

- Why did you get rid of all your "secular" music?
- Why is it important to you to let people know you don't see certain kinds of movies or are committed to a daily quiet time?
- Why have you posted on your social media page the picture you took with some ethnically different child?

Don't get me wrong. Convictions are great, along with adoption and moving into impoverished neighborhoods. But the moment these things become identity insignias, we have passed from abiding to performing and are on a collision course with weary.

So in an insane act of grace, Jesus picks up his pipe once again and invites good, moral people to go from performing to abiding. "Come to me, all you who are weary and burdened, and I will give you rest," he says as he beckons.

The Greek word Matthew uses here for *come* is in the imperative mood. When you think of an imperative, think command. Jesus is more than inviting; he is lovingly commanding us to step off the treadmill of morality and to rest in him. John 15:4 (ESV) captures the spirit of Jesus' invitation: "Abide in me, and I in you. As the branch cannot bear fruit by itself, unless it abides in the vine, neither can you, unless you abide in me." If we want a life rich with fruit that blesses others, it doesn't happen by *doing* more, but by *abiding* more, by coming to Jesus and resting in relationship with him.

TAKE

Coming to Jesus isn't enough. In Matthew 11:29, Jesus says, "Take my yoke upon you and learn from me, for I am gentle and humble in heart, and you will find rest for your souls." Jesus' words are perplexing. He's talking to people worn-out by religion and invites them to come to him for rest. *Okay, I'm tracking with you. Love this.* But now, "Take my yoke upon you"? *Really? Like, it would make more sense if Jesus said, "Take a vacation"*—not, "Take my yoke upon you."

A yoke was a contraption farmers used when it was time for animals to work. They'd put a pair of oxen together, fit them with the yoke, and take them out to the field for a day of labor. Yoke is work. See the irony? Jesus says, "I can see you're worn-out; come to me, and let's get yoked together so we can work.

We'll talk some more about this in the next section, but it's important to point out that abiding in God's performance-free love is not devoid of work. I sometimes get concerned with Christians who so overreact to the legalism of previous generations that they send the message that the Christian life requires no labor or work. There's no way you can read Jesus' invitation and get that. Yoke means work. Or consider Paul. Read his letters. He's constantly telling Christ followers to put off certain things and put on other things (Colossians 3:5–17). To the Philippians, he flat-out tells them to "work out your salvation" (Philippians 2:12). And in reflecting on his time with the Thessalonians, Paul said he worked night and day (1 Thessalonians 2:9). The way of Jesus is not about drifting through this world in a comatose state, waiting on him to do everything. There's work involved.

Like the moralist, we do work, but unlike them, followers of Jesus are not independent contractors. We give and work in tandem with Jesus and out of joy for all he's done for us.

Jesus unpacks this principle of work and God's performance-free love in Matthew 22. He tells the story of a king who prepared a wedding feast for his son. The king sends his servants to invite as many as possible. None come at first, so he sends another wave of servants. Not only do people refuse to come, but they turn violent on the servants, beating and even killing them. Finally, the king tells the last wave of servants to go out into the streets and invite all they can, bad and good.

Walking into the wedding feast filled with the unusual suspects, the king's attention is grabbed by a man who isn't wearing wedding clothes. This man is probably too poor to rent a tux and is just there for the food. Makes sense, but what happens next is baffling: The king asks, "How did you get in here without wedding clothes, friend?" The man is speechless. So the king orders this man not only to be thrown out of the reception, but to be tied up and cast outside into darkness—into a place "where there will be weeping and gnashing of teeth" (Matthew 22:11–14).

This seems a little harsh. Kick out a poor man you invited to your wedding feast and send him to a place of suffering? Huh? The only way to make sense of this is to see the event through first-century eyes. In Jesus' day, the father of the groom was responsible not only for the food at the wedding feast but also for the wedding clothes. Weddings had a certain dress code, and the father supplied the outfits to all who attended. Who wouldn't want this tradition to continue today (unless you are the parents of the groom)? So this man's tuxedo had already been provided. His presence at the wedding feast, dressed in his own garb, communicated a staunch refusal to accept the king's clothes. He thought he could make it in on his own terms, dressed in his old outfit.

Jesus is driving home a message he has hammered throughout Matthew's gospel: God's performance-free love cannot be attained through our own attempts. At some point, we must accept King Jesus' gracious invitation to come to him—and do so with the outfit he supplies. Life in the kingdom means I come out of my old clothes of performance and receive the new ones of abiding in Christ.

But there's something else in this story that helps us digest Jesus' invitation in Matthew 11. The setting is a wedding feast. When those of you who are married think of your reception, words like *joy* and *gladness* come to mind. It was likely a time of laughter and dancing—much joy. Life in God's kingdom involves work—"take my yoke"—but the work we do is not of the performance variety, but is done out of sheer joy for the One who saved and redeemed us. This completely changes how we view things like sharing our faith with others.

Evangelism is a hard subject for Christ followers. Who

hasn't experienced sweaty palms and a lump in their throat when they've felt the nudge of the Spirit to share their faith with others? I have. For many, we've reduced witnessing to the category of the obligatory. It has become duty when it should be joy.

Think of your favorite experiences—maybe the best meal you've ever had or the perfect movie. What did you do not long after you left the restaurant or movie theater? You called your friends and told them they *had* to order a certain meal, see a particular movie, or read that extraordinary book. You witnessed, but you did so out of a joy birthed in the wonderful experience you felt. It's one of life's universal truths that we share with others what brings us joy. If we know the joy of abiding in Christ, of having our sins washed and forgiven, of daily grace and mercy, then we'll do the work of sharing that joy with others. Taking Christ's yoke upon us is not obligatory; it's joy.

LEARN

Next, Jesus invites us to learn from him. The Greek word for *learn* derives from the same group of words translated as "disciple." A disciple is a learner. Jesus wants us to learn from him, and to do this, we have to constantly look to Jesus as our example. In his three years of following Jesus, Peter must have really grasped this idea because he later wrote, "To this you were called, because Christ suffered for you, leaving you an example, that you should follow in his steps" (1 Peter 2:21).

It's hard to consistently look to Jesus, isn't it? In times of prosperity, we tend to look at ourselves or our possessions and away from Jesus. In times of difficulty, we can become so inebriated with our circumstances that we look away from the Lord of our situation. Fixing our eyes on Jesus cuts against the grain of fallen humanity.

My son's blood disease meant he had to have his blood drawn a lot. At one of his first appointments, I could see he was getting really anxious and was on the verge of bailing. I sat him on my lap and said to the nurse, "This could be against protocol, but I was wondering if you could draw my blood first, just so my son can see it's not so bad." She obliged, found the vein in my arm, sprayed some of the stuff on it, stuck a needle in my arm, and drew some blood. My son was taking in this whole scene, and when I asked him if he was ready, he took a deep breath and whispered to himself, *I can do this*. The nurse found his vein, sprayed the stuff, and drew blood. When it was over, a huge smile stretched across my son's face, and he said, "I did it, Dad!" Where did his strength come from to conquer his fears? He looked to Dad and learned from me.

Abiding in God's amazing love is not pain-free. Live long enough, and fear and anxiety will come knocking. People headaches, financial difficulties, health crises, and more will probably show up at your door. When this happens, we need to learn to look to "Jesus, the pioneer and perfecter of faith. For the joy set before him he endured the cross, scorning its shame, and sat down at the right hand of the throne of God" (Hebrews 12:2).

A CUSTOM-MADE BURDEN

Jesus ends his invitation to those worn-out by morality and performance with these words: "My yoke is easy and my burden is light" (Matthew 11:30). Talk about a great exchange. Instead of trying to enter the wedding feast of the kingdom in our old sweaty clothes, Jesus offers a different path, and this path is easy and light.

The word for *easy* is a bit deceptive. In the Greek, the word means "custom-made, or tailor-made." Whenever an ox needed a yoke, its owner never grabbed one "off the rack"—a one-size-fits-all yoke. Instead, a carpenter measured the ox's neck and custom-made a yoke to fit him. This way, the yoke wouldn't be too heavy or chafe its neck. The custom-made yoke became bearable for the specific ox.

Jesus says, "My yoke is easy." As the divine Carpenter, Jesus knows you inside and out. He knows what you can handle and what you cannot. He knows what you can bear and how far is too far. Armed with this knowledge, Jesus customizes the yokes and trials of our lives so there's nothing we go through that we cannot handle.

Does life seem a little heavy to you right now? Do you feel burdened and weighed down? May Jesus' invitation give you fresh joy. You and Jesus are yoked together. He's in this with you, and there's nothing—I mean *nothing*—that comes on you that you can't handle. You got this. May we accept Jesus' invitation and rest in God's amazing love.

grilled grace

WHY YOUR FAILURE IS NEVER FINAL

It was tricky trying to find the guilty party in a lynching—America's earliest organized terrorist campaign. Lynchings tended to be spontaneous, and sure, while the initial aggressors barged their way into jailhouses and accosted the accused with no thought to due process, you may not want to be so quick as to only single *them* out for culpability. Photographs of lynchings are gruesome, with the most grotesque image reserved not for the charred, mutilated corpse left dangling from some Southern tree but for the masses of people who joined in the festivities, eating their pimento cheese sandwiches and sipping their mint juleps as if they were at a Sunday afternoon picnic. Is not the latter group just as culpable as the former? Scholar Robert Schreiter agrees, making a case that bystanders cannot escape culpability in instances of injustice when they had it within their means to act but chose to look the other way, or in this case to look on while they enjoyed their lunch.[1]

Something in us bristles at Schreiter's suggestion. Sure, we understand that the white woman who willingly slept with a black man but in a fit of panic lied and accused him of rape to protect her image should be punished. And certainly the men who circumvented due process, paying no thought to the American edict of "innocent until proven guilty," should be punished as well. Maybe we could even cosign on the culpability of the policemen, whose job was to protect the accused from the mob, yet they opened the jailhouse doors and allowed the mob to have its way. But should we also blame the hundreds, if not thousands, who just sat on the lawn to watch the spectacle? Were not many of these people moral, upstanding citizens who even professed to be followers of Christ? Should they receive a similar fate as the woman who lied or the men who hung the victim? Mass culpability is a difficult dilemma.

WHO KILLED JESUS?

We encounter a similar dilemma when we consider the death of Jesus. Theologian James Cone in *The Cross and the Lynching Tree* compared the death of Jesus to the lynchings of the late nineteenth and early twentieth centuries. Think about it. Like the lynching victims, Jesus was arrested by an angry mob in Gethsemane and falsely accused by several witnesses, with very little thought to due process. Passive government officials, like Pilate, who could have intervened and demanded a stop to the whole thing simply turned the other way while a bloodthirsty and fickle crowd that had just shouted, "Hosanna to the Son of David!" now demanded, "Crucify him!" And the death of Jesus, in a way eerily similar to the lynchings of the American South, was no private matter. It was very public.

All this and more leave us wondering, *Who is at fault for the death of Jesus?* Was it the angry religious mob, the lying "witnesses," or the passive Gentile leaders? Should Jesus' death be laid on the shoulders of Judas, Jesus' handpicked disciple who sold him out for thirty pieces of silver, or should we also indict the other eleven disciples, especially when ten of them abandoned Christ at the cross? Who exactly is responsible for the death of Jesus?

As Matthew parades out the cast of characters involved

in the death of Jesus, a stunning picture emerges. Of course, there are the religious leaders who finally got their hands on Jesus in Gethsemane. But there's also Pilate, the passive Gentile government official who had it in his power to let Jesus go yet looked the other way. Then there's the crowd that shouted their verdict, "Crucify him!" Finally, we have the disciples, many of whom grew up in good, moral homes where the Scriptures were taught, and yet one betrays Jesus and the others scurry for cover. Their flight was as strong as Peter's verbal denial. Through it all, Matthew sketches a surprisingly composite picture of Jesus' killer—everyone. As the great preacher Dr. E. K. Bailey said in his legendary sermon "Confessions of an Ex-Crossmaker," we are all guilty of the death of Christ.

This is a truth almost impossible to digest. The Bible doesn't just stop at the impossibility of people entering heaven on their own merits, even if those efforts are broadly considered to be good. No, the Bible carries moralism to an unthinkable conclusion: "Moral" people were responsible for the killing of Jesus. It smacks of being a bit oxymoronic, doesn't it—moral murderers?

Our good deeds hammered the nails into the hands and feet of Christ, pinning him to the cross. The only way to make sense of this concept is to understand the nature of sin. At its core, sin is acting independently of God. Sin is choosing life on our own terms. Sin says, "I've got this, so leave me alone."

Where I tend to get mixed up is to think the promiscuous and the chaste are two radically different groups of people. *Not so fast*, the Bible argues. If a person is sexually restraining himself or herself in order to find value and meaning on their own terms, they are just as culpable for the murder of Jesus as a porn star is, because both have chosen to act independently of God and reject the performance-free love he offers.

Matthew wasn't the first to convict the world of murdering Jesus. Some 750 years before Matthew, God banged his gavel and rendered his verdict. Using the image of wayward, independent sheep in his closing argument of universal guilt when it came to the execution of his Son, Jesus Christ, God communicated this message through Isaiah: "We all, like sheep, have gone astray, each of us has turned to our own way; and the LORD has laid on him *the iniquity of us all*" (Isaiah 53:6, emphasis mine). In this one verse, God shows the nature of sin (independence) and the devastating consequences of our independence (the death of Jesus). Who acted independently? Everyone. From the irreligious to the religious, we are *all* responsible for the death of Jesus—even moral people.

IT'S COMPLICATED

Why would Matthew and other biographers include Peter in the death narrative of Jesus? If the cross is only for the so-called bad, then Peter's actions on the eve of Jesus' crucifixion have no relevance. But if Matthew is right that *all the world* is in need of the cross—even moral people—then Peter's inclusion in the narrative is necessary. Why did God insist all four gospel writers document Peter's disowning of Jesus? I believe it's because God wanted it on record for all of human history: Even moral people played an active role in the killing of Jesus and are in grave need of the cross. Look at Matthew 26:69–75:

> Now Peter was sitting out in the courtyard, and a servant girl came to him. "You also were with Jesus of Galilee," she said.
>
> But he denied it before them all. "I don't know what you're talking about," he said.

Then he went out to the gateway, where another servant girl saw him and said to the people there, "This fellow was with Jesus of Nazareth."

He denied it again, with an oath: "I don't know the man!"

After a little while, those standing there went up to Peter and said, "Surely you are one of them; your accent gives you away."

Then he began to call down curses, and he swore to them, "I don't know the man!"

Immediately a rooster crowed. Then Peter remembered the word Jesus had spoken: "Before the rooster crows, you will disown me three times." And he went outside and wept bitterly.

Peter's actions are surprising. This was the guy who just a few chapters earlier had said Jesus was the long-awaited Messiah—the Son of the living God (Matthew 16:16). Then, not long after this, it was Peter who was favored by Jesus to stand with him, Elijah, and Moses on the mount of transfiguration. Overwhelmed with excitement, he must have started talking too much, because God cuts in and pretty much tells him to keep quiet and listen to his Son, Jesus. Who can forget the stormy night at sea when Peter took a few steps on the water? Now I know he gets a bad rap for sinking, but let's give our boy Pete some credit. He was, after all, the only one courageous enough to get out of the boat. And remember, Peter is a part of Jesus' inner circle—along with James and John—who just a few moments before the disowning was given VIP access into one of the most emotionally exhausting moments in the life of our Savior.

Now this same guy who got the answers right, walked on water, and stood with Jesus in the peaks and valleys ends up denying any connection he had with him. I'm a little thrown by Peter's actions. Talk about complicated.

Let's be fair, we're all pretty complicated, aren't we? Moses was. There are times we catch Moses pleading with God to be patient with Israel, only to turn around and, out of impatience with these same people, strike a rock in anger. How about David? He's known as the sweet psalmist of Israel, and he's also known for his adultery and murder. Then there's his son Solomon, probably the most complicated person in the Bible. Solomon is called the wisest person who ever lived, but this same man acted in a completely foolish manner with women. It's complicated.

How about you? Ever been shocked by a thought or by some of your actions? Sin makes complicated messes out of all of us. Even by our own standards, we're not as moral as we'd like to think we are. Peter's disowning should give us pause before we say what we will and won't do. We're all complicated messes in need of daily grace.

This episode in the life of Peter should also make us question our use of the phrase "falling into sin." I could see Peter denying knowing Jesus once and then autocorrecting, but he doesn't. Three times Peter denies knowing Jesus, with each denial strengthening his grip on sin. His first denial seems innocent. You can almost see Peter shrugging his shoulders and shaking his head when accused of being with Jesus. Almost nonchalantly, he says, "I don't know what you're talking about." Things, however, get ratcheted up when he's asked again about his relationship with Jesus. This time, Matthew says that Peter not only denies knowing Jesus, but he does so with an oath. He probably swears by heaven and earth while denouncing any ties with Christ. Finally, things reach a crescendo when the bystanders express with certainty Peter's affiliation with Jesus.

To borrow a line from the hip-hop community, Peter "turns up" and not only denies knowing Jesus, but he does so while cursing himself and swearing. One commentator suggests Peter is cursing Jesus. In antiquity, if a person wanted to convince another that he was not affiliated with a certain group or individual, he would curse the ones he had been accused of having a relationship with. It's possible Peter's final disowning of Jesus includes cursing him.

The progression of Peter's sin (I should say, the digression) confronts us with an ugly truth: Sin is never static. There is no cruise control when it comes to sin. The longer we stay committed to our sin, the more entangled we become and the further we drift from Jesus. Just look at Peter's physical drift. When the scene opens, he's sitting in the courtyard (Matthew 26:69). One denial later, he retreats to the entrance (verse 71). Finally, faced with the shame of his sin, "he went outside and wept bitterly" (verse 75). Each sin moves Peter further and further from Jesus.

Does Jesus seem far from you? I've had seasons in my life when it felt like Jesus was a long plane ride away. The writer of Hebrews says Jesus is the same yesterday, today, and forever (Hebrews 13:8). Theologians use this verse to support what is called the "immutability" of Christ. What we mean by immutability is the fact that Jesus never changes. He's the same. So if he feels far from us, it's not Jesus who drifted; it's us. Sin causes us to moonwalk away from our Savior.

THE FUMES OF FAILURE

Thank God Peter didn't disown Christ in the digital age. Can you imagine someone recording Pete's threefold disowning, cursing and all, then uploading it onto the Internet for all the world to see? Our boy would be through. No more ministry. No more preaching. Google Peter, and the site with the most hits would be the one of him lying and cussing. The Internet is known for a lot of things, and it's too bad that grace isn't one of them.

This passage is a really dark one, which is why I have a hard time with Matthew's version of Peter's sin. I remember preparing to preach on this text, and being at a loss, wondering where the hope was. It's here that I'm thankful for John, because as John takes in Peter's denial, he includes a little detail: "Now the servants and officers had made a *charcoal fire*, because it was cold, and they were standing and warming themselves. Peter also was with them, standing and warming himself" (John 18:18 ESV, emphasis mine). John adds a wrinkle to the setting of Peter's disowning of Jesus—a charcoal fire.

Run a search on the phrase "charcoal fire," and you'll discover it's only used twice in the Bible, both times by John in reference to Peter. The second time John uses the phrase is three chapters later in John 21. Still rankled by his sin, Peter recruits some of the disciples to join him for a night of fishing, and they catch nothing. Some hours later, as day was just beginning to dawn, a man called out from the beach, asking if they had caught anything. Probably annoyed by the question, the men tell him no, to which the man asks them to cast on the right side of the boat. They humor him and end up catching so much fish that it takes a concerted effort to bring their nets in. Then it hits Peter. He's seen this before. It's Jesus! Diving headfirst into the water, Peter swims ashore. Emerging from the sea, the disciples "saw a *charcoal fire* in place, with fish laid out on it, and bread" (John 21:9 ESV, emphasis mine). With the smell of the charcoal fire wafting in the air, Jesus asks Peter three times if he loves him. After each response, Jesus tells him to feed his sheep. Jesus' message is laced with hope: *I haven't given up on you.* What grace!

There's a connection between our memories and our sense

of smell. My grandmother was known for her fried apples. She has been dead for years, but whenever I smell fried apples, I see her sweet face. She loved waking up early and making them for me. The scent of fried apples ushers in a flood of memories, and before I know it, a tear is dripping down my face.

What fried apples are to my childhood, a charcoal fire is to Peter's sin. When Peter first catches the whiff of the charcoal smell, his mind had to have wandered back to his sin of denying that he knew Jesus. And if you think Jesus just so happened to cook with charcoal fire, I've got a skyscraper I'd love to sell you in the Atlantic Ocean. Jesus intentionally cooks breakfast on a charcoal fire because he wants Peter to remember his sin.

CHARCOAL GRACE

Grace is not spiritual amnesia. Grace is charcoal fires and rearview mirrors. There's a reason the rearview mirrors in our cars are smaller than the windshield. They weren't meant to be stared at. You glance at rearview mirrors because they give perspective for what's behind you so you can make the best decisions moving forward.

Grace is a rearview mirror. No, we don't stare at the sin of our past, but we shouldn't forget it altogether. In my own travels with Jesus, I've found it helpful to take a glance at some of the ugly things I've done on the road behind me. It keeps me humble and propels me forward. God wanted Israel to look at her rearview mirror to catch a whiff of the charcoal. He reminded them on more than one occasion to not forget their days in Egypt and how the Lord brought them out. Paul took a peek at his own rearview mirror. I can see him wince as he remembers the days he spent persecuting Christians. Every now and then, Paul would call himself the worst of sinners (e.g., 1 Timothy 1:15).

John Newton was known for smelling God's charcoal grace. Every year when he celebrated his spiritual birthday, the day he came to faith in Jesus Christ, he reflected on his days as a cussing, sexually immoral, slave-trading sailor. He sighed deeply over his sin, yet celebrated God's amazing grace. To know John Newton was to see grace and humility in real time. Some of the most gracious people I know are those who have a habit of glancing back in the rearview mirror of life.

I've spent my life straining to see the multiethnic church become the new normal in our world. Addressing issues of race is like pressing against a wound that hasn't completely healed. As Edward Gilbreath writes in his book *Reconciliation Blues*, the problem with those of us who build bridges between ethnicities is we often get stepped on.[2] I've seen more than my share of colleagues who got tired of the abuse, burned out, and turned bitter.

Not John Perkins. Well into the winter years of his life, Dr. Perkins is the personification of grace and humility. Growing up in Mississippi, he was once unjustly thrown in jail and tortured by white officers. Lying on the jail floor, he felt as though his anger was on the precipice of bitterness. Shocked over his flowering hatred for whites, Dr. Perkins decided to let love win. Now when he's tempted toward bitterness, he remembers the jail cell in Mississippi where he saw the reflection of his own sin, and he chooses grace and joy.

People in tune with God's grace end up being incredibly gracious. When we really come to terms with our failure to perform—to measure up to God's standards—and are in touch with our need for fresh, daily grace, we can't help but extend grace to others. It really is true: People basking in performance-free love display this same love to others.

Don't waste your past. No, I'm not asking you to brood over

it. Remember, your past is a rearview mirror. If you stared at it, you'd wreck your car and never reach God's destination for your life. But don't bury the sin of your past either. Glance at the betrayal but keep moving. Catch a whiff of the breach of integrity, but press forward. Remember the failure, and use it to dispense greater helpings of grace and humility toward others. Don't waste your past.

FAILURE ISN'T FINAL

With the smell of charcoal still drifting in the air, Jesus asks Peter three times if he loves him. Everything in the scene points to an awkward moment. The charcoal fire reminds Peter of his sin of disowning Jesus, and as he's daydreaming about the worst night ever, Jesus cuts in and wants to know if Peter loves him? Awkward.

Each time, Peter affirms his love for Jesus, and then Jesus responds, "Feed my sheep." Talk about grace. When Jesus says three times "feed my sheep," it is his way of saying, *Peter, you failed, but I'm not finished with you.* A few weeks later, this disowning, cussing-out-Jesus Peter would preach to a large crowd on the day of Pentecost and see God use him to bring three thousand people into the kingdom and birth a new thing called the church. Peter's life screams, *Failure isn't final.*

The cross is a place of fresh beginnings. Paul wrote, "When you were dead in your sins and in the uncircumcision of your flesh, God made you alive with Christ. He forgave us all our sins, having canceled the charge of our legal indebtedness, which stood against us and condemned us; he has taken it away, nailing it to the cross" (Colossians 2:13–14).

"Legal indebtedness" was the Roman version of a credit report. It listed what you owed, and your signature authenticated the document, holding you legally responsible for paying your debts. Paul uses this image to point us to the grace of Jesus Christ on the cross. All of our sins, everything we have ever done to break God's heart, have gone on a spiritual credit report. But on the cross, Paul says, our record of debt was canceled.

The English equivalent of the Greek word Paul uses for "canceled" is *expunged*. Legally speaking, if you have something expunged from your record, it's not just removed; it's removed in such a way that it is as if you never did it. This actually happened to a friend of mine who had committed a crime, which if it were to remain on his record, he'd never vote again. But mercifully, he had his record expunged, and now the privileges of voting and the full rights of citizenship are his. His legal indebtedness, his record of debt, was canceled, expunged.

This is what Jesus did for Peter and for each one of us. Over a charcoal fire, Peter is reminded of his sin and also receives the grace of Jesus to move forward. How is this disowning and cussing man able to preach God's Word just a few weeks later? His record is expunged through the cross, and he is granted full rights as a citizen of the kingdom and a child of the King.

Why are we still here? Why does God still use us, even though we were accomplices to the murder of his Son, Jesus? Our sins were expunged, not through our white-knuckled, try-harder morality, but through the death of Jesus Christ. We call that grace. Go ahead, take a whiff of your past, but rest in the grace of Jesus, who has removed your sins as far as the east is from the west.

the greatest performance act in history

THE RESURRECTION IS FOR US

Up until several years ago, I guarantee that you hadn't heard the name Henrietta Lacks. If it still doesn't sound familiar to you, I understand, but please get to know her, because chances are she has literally touched either you or someone you love.

Henrietta died in 1951 of ovarian cancer. What brought her to prominence, though, was the fact that her cells became the first on record to grow continuously outside her body. Seizing this medical breakthrough, doctors harvested her cells and used them to come up with a cure for polio and as a tool for fighting cancer and AIDS. Her cells have traveled to every country on earth and even took a trip into outer space. In the medical community, Henrietta Lacks is simply known as HeLa, and as HeLa, she's posthumously improved the quality of a lot of people's lives.

A dead woman whose cells live, and through those living cells she spawns life for others.

While Henrietta (aka HeLa) is a medical phenomenon, there's a Greater One. His name is Jesus Christ, who died and rose again, and through his life, we can have life—real life. Because God did the performing for us, not only by sending his Son, Jesus, to die on the cross for us, but also by raising him from the dead three days later, you and I can rest in the work already done for us. There is no greater performance in human history than what happened for us early on that Sunday morning, and it is through God and through Jesus' performance for us that you and I can have hope and life-altering transformation. He died to save us from sin and death, from lives blind to truth and unimaginable love—and you know what else? He died to save us from ourselves, from our own harried attempts to be good enough. The resurrection wipes this notion clean off the table. Because Jesus is the *only* One who is good enough, the only perfect One, we don't have to be. Instead, we can *receive* his goodness through the gift of his life, death, and resurrection. We can stop trying to perform our way into God's heart and start abiding with the One who completed the greatest performance act of all so we could be called his children.

EXPECT THE INCREDIBLE

Like any good story, the best part of Matthew's gospel is at the end. He waits until the last chapter to unfold the tale of Jesus' resurrection, and as he does, we see two women hurriedly making their way to the grave of Jesus. In Mark's telling of the narrative, he explains why these two Marys have traveled to the tomb of Jesus: They've come to anoint his body with spices, preserving it for burial (Mark 16:1).

Now on the one hand, their actions are completely admirable. Family and friends of the deceased often served as modern-day morticians, dressing and preparing the body for burial. This is why these two women have come—to perform a final duty for their departed rabbi.

On the other hand, doesn't it seem a bit weird they are there, expecting to see a dead Jesus? I mean, didn't they hear him talk on more than one occasion of his imminent death and subsequent resurrection? These women have come to the tomb of Jesus out of devotion, yet there isn't a hint of resurrection expectation on their part. They've come armed with burial spices rather than hope-filled expectancy. Duty devoid of hope is a dangerous thing.

There's no way I can wag my finger at these two, though. I know what it's like to give the obligatory performance without the slightest glimmer of expectation. I have a feeling you can relate to the two Marys and to me as well. Ever prayed a big prayer while thinking somewhere deep within, *There's no way this is going to happen?* Or given money through gritted teeth, feeling the pain of your "generosity" as you responded to the preacher's recitation of Malachi 3:10, all the while thinking, *Yeah, right,* to that whole bit about God pouring out such a blessing that you won't have room to receive it? In each of these instances (and more), we bring our own embalming fluid and burial spices to our actions.

When I was a little boy living in Atlanta, my dad had his briefcase stolen while at a rental car counter in Los Angeles. My younger brother suggested we should ask God to return Dad's briefcase. All of us around the dinner table had more than a share of *yeah, right* that evening as we prayed. But during the next several months, my kid brother refused to let it go, demanding we pray every evening for God to return the briefcase. Even my dad had to confess that his expectation was waning.

Well, wouldn't you know it, about two months later, a man called my dad to tell him he found a briefcase in the dumpster, opened it, saw my dad's card, and called, wondering where he wanted him to ship the briefcase. When Dad gave us the news, all but one of us was surprised. It's nearly impossible to shock the expectant. I guess that's what explains the two Marys' wonderment when the angel announces that the one they were looking for—Jesus—was no longer there. Their shock revealed a lack of expectancy.

A performance-free love means nothing without a future hope, and our hope is based on the empty tomb—the resurrection of Jesus Christ. Take this away, and we are left with a joyless, plotless performance at best, where like these Marys, we show up and fulfill our obligation out of a stoic, perfunctory have-to instead of a joyful, otherworldly get-to.

Expectancy is tied not to optimism, but to hope. There is a difference. People are optimistic about things that are uncertain, like lottery tickets, their prospects of getting married, or doing well on a test. There's no guarantee your number will hit or he'll put a ring on it. And while I'm not advocating for a "glass half empty," negative outlook on life, hope is so much more. The writer of Hebrews tells us that hope is something fixed in reality (Hebrews 6:18–20), and that reality is God and his Son, Jesus Christ. The empty tomb is not some nice myth, but a hope-filled historical reality. What the vacancy of Jesus' tomb bequeaths is a fixed hope. Just as he fulfilled his word once in rising from the grave, so we can count on him fulfilling his word by coming back again. Christians have more than optimism; we have hope—real hope.

This changes the game when it comes to how we steward life. The Bible paints a picture of hope that transcends feelings and spills over into actions. My hope in Jesus and his empty tomb and second coming colors how I care for and interact with others. My hope in Jesus gives me pause in how I steward the money he's given me. My hope in Jesus won't let me dismiss the poor and downtrodden.

THE RESURRECTION IS FOR US

As the two women approach the tomb, they are immediately faced with a dilemma—the stone is still there, sealing the tomb. What's more, the Jewish leaders had been concerned about a conspiracy to steal the corpse of Jesus, so they asked for a special guard to secure the premise. With all this security, what were the two Marys to do?

They don't have long to come up with a plan, because according to Matthew 28:2, a great earthquake occurs, with an angel of the Lord coming from heaven and rolling back the stone. These women go from grief-stricken to awe-filled in the span of two verses.

Now this raises questions like, *Why did an angel need to come and roll away the stone?* It wasn't as if Jesus was pacing back and forth inside the tomb, waiting for the angel to get him out of there. This is Jesus we're talking about. If he wanted out, he could've done that himself. The angel came not to let Jesus out, but to let these two Marys in. The resurrection wasn't for Jesus; it was for us.

This is how Paul and the early leaders of the church understood the resurrection. Paul spent a whole chapter in his letter to the Corinthians talking about the resurrection and its foundational implications for our lives. Because Jesus rose from the grave, Paul argues, life now has meaning. The resurrection of Jesus Christ not only verifies his indestructible nature but also offers this same indestructible gift of a performance-free love to us. What else could Paul have meant when he wrote these words?

The perishable must clothe itself with the imperishable, and the mortal with immortality. When the perishable has been clothed with the imperishable, and the mortal with immortality, then the saying that is written will come true: "Death has been swallowed up in victory."

> *"Where, O death, is your victory?*
> *Where, O death, is your sting?"*

The sting of death is sin, and the power of sin is the law. But thanks be to God! He gives us the victory through our Lord Jesus Christ

1 Corinthians 15:53–57

Because Jesus Christ conquered death through the resurrection and therefore became indestructible, all of us who are in Christ will conquer death. Our perishable bodies will be made imperishable, all because of the resurrection of Jesus Christ.

All of this is made possible through his love.

What does this mean for us as we go about today's affairs? Everything. If this life is not final, then you and I are a part of a grand metanarrative that's so much more than work, money, clothes, and status. Life now has a rich, textured meaning.

All of us are searching for meaning. We want to matter, and that's a good thing. A part of what it means to be made in the image of God is to have an unfettered desire to leave our mark for good on this earth. The apathetic life is not worth living. So each day, all of us in our own way set about our journeys toward significance. The problem is that most of us take the broad path, and the path of choice is moralism—the path these two Marys took.

But the women in our narrative show us that duty detached from a grand metanarrative is devoid of long-term joy; it's drudgery, a bag filled with burial spices. It's also plotless.

Roberta Flack put voice to this maddening quest for meaning in her song *Compared to What*. In one of the verses, she talks of sitting in church listening to the preacher as she sleeps and nods, "tryin' to duck the wrath of God." Fighting sleep while trying to make sense of the preacher's rant, she calls him "some kind of nut, tryin' to make it real, but compared to what?" Embedded in her sarcasm is the universal question of meaning.

A generation after Roberta Flack sang these words, we postmoderns continued to ask the ancient question of meaning. No longer amused by the fairy-tale sitcom solving life's biggest dilemmas in a half-hour time frame, we began to turn our attention to shows emphasizing "reality." Most cultural anthropologists agree it was *Seinfeld* that represented a major transition in television. In the pilot for the show, Jerry Seinfeld said he wanted to present something preoccupied with nothing. And we tuned in—in record numbers—because finally we found some solace in our frustrated attempts at life detached from a master narrative. In its wake, *Seinfeld* inspired the reality-show genre of television, giving birth to *Keeping Up with the Kardashians*, *Jersey Shore*, and a host of other shows that proudly were also much ado about nothing.

But we still have a problem. The temporary nature of these shows exposes their inability to satisfy the longings of our hearts. Just as the fairy-tale sitcoms couldn't quite do it, neither can reality—or good works. We long for something more.

The resurrection of Jesus Christ is our final stop on the journey into meaning. Paul points out to the Corinthians that the resurrection of Jesus Christ is the ultimate victory over sin and death. Jesus became the ransom for our sins on that Friday afternoon, and Jesus conquered our sin, once and for all, on that Sunday morning. Jesus did it all. This is truly good news, because we no longer have to labor through white-knuckled morality to feel good about ourselves and our place in the world. The empty tomb takes you and me from striving to abiding. Because Christ has done the work, we are free to rest in him. Because Christ has conquered, we are now free.

FEAR TRANSFORMED INTO FAITH

The resurrection of Jesus Christ is all about change. First, we see the empty tomb literally changing the ground the women stood on. Matthew documents an earthquake happening, right when the stone is rolled away. Following the resurrected Lord is not about adding him to your already hectic life, but it demands unsettling the very foundations you stood on prior to encountering the risen Lord. If there is not a seismic shift in how you steward money, navigate relationships, view sexuality, and engage the less fortunate, it's worth asking if you've really encountered the risen Lord. Truly, the gospel changes everything, disrupting old paradigms and offering new ones.

Not only was the ground changed, but so were these women. Matthew observes, "The women hurried away from the tomb, afraid yet filled with joy, and ran to tell his disciples" (28:8). The two Marys came to the tomb out of duty, filled with grief and assuming they'd find a dead Jesus. Now they leave totally changed, filled with great joy and expectancy as they run to tell the disciples the good news.

It's impossible to come to the empty tomb and leave unchanged. This is an important lesson both Marys teach us. On the one hand, the kingdom of God is filled with sinners in daily need of abundant grace from an all-merciful God. On the other hand, the only real assurance that salvation is genuinely invading our hearts is a life in which we become increasingly transformed into the image of Jesus. Saying I know Jesus isn't enough; my affections and actions should be flowering more and more into the image of God.

This is what the resurrection is about—change.

But we also see purpose. Having exchanged their burial spices for joy, the two Marys are commissioned by the angel to "go quickly and tell his disciples: 'He has risen from the dead'" (Matthew 28:7). They've been invited into the grand narrative of Jesus and sent out with an unlikely purpose: to be God's witnesses in the world of his resurrection work.

I call this unlikely because if you know anything about women in the first-century Roman world, you'd see how preposterous it was for them to serve as the first witnesses to the most incredible story. Women weren't allowed to serve as witnesses in a Roman court because they were perceived to be in-credible. The fact these women are the first witnesses to the resurrection actually adds credibility to the story. If Matthew and his cohorts were making this up, you would either lie and have men be the first witnesses or leave out the whole "women bit" altogether.

But not only does having women serve as witnesses to the resurrection grant credence to the story; it also shows a humorous God who delights in calling the most unlikely into his grand narrative. Just moments before, they were two women about to perform a typical duty carried out by women, and now they have a larger-than-life purpose nobody will believe. This is what God does repeatedly throughout human history, and sometimes I think he does it just for laughs.

The disciples instigated laughs and ridicule from the religious elite because they were "unlearned" men who had not matriculated through the normal, credible channels of religious education, and yet these men became the leaders of the church, turning the world on its ear. And let's not forget that all but one cowered in fear when Jesus was taken into custody. One betrayed Jesus; another denied knowing Jesus; most abandoned Jesus. Not long later, however, we find them boldly proclaiming the name of Jesus, even dying for their faith. What transformed them from fear to faith? The empty tomb.

Don't you see the picture Matthew is painting of the resurrection? Over and over again, we are introduced to people who fail to measure up and who perform miserably, but once they catch a glimpse of the empty tomb and the resurrection power of Jesus, they not only are captivated by his performance-free love but also share that same love boldly with others. From the two Marys who expected to embalm a dead Jesus, to the disciples who abandoned Jesus on the cross and returned to their former way of life, to you and me, the message is the same: None of us are good enough. What qualifies us to be used in any way possible is God's amazing love worked through the greatest miracle ever performed—the resurrection of Jesus Christ.

Where is true meaning found in life? Jesus said we catch glimpses of it when we give and not just receive, when we forgive others of their trespasses against us, and when we, like the two Marys, announce to others the good news of Jesus Christ. The source for all of these meaningful actions and more is the resurrected Jesus. Four words can change not only the ground under your feet but also the way you approach life: "He is not here."

living in and reflecting God's performance-free love

the most difficult math problem in the world

PRACTICING FORGIVENESS

> *"I do not say to you, up to seven times,*
> *but up to seventy times seven."*
> **Jesus, in Matthew 18:22 NASB**

> *Unless we look the beast in the eye, we find it has*
> *an uncanny habit of returning to hold us hostage.*
> **Bishop Desmond Tutu**

How do I really know I'm a Christian? What proof do I have that I am truly living in God's performance-free love? Matthew addresses these foundational questions as he writes to his religious audience. See, for Matthew, he's not just concerned with showing us the better way of abiding in God's love; he's also interested in how this potent love emanates from our lives and pierces the world around us.

Take the issue of forgiveness. Nothing lays us bare, exposing who we really are, like opposition and difficulty. Struggle often serves as a probe that reveals what's well beneath the surface of our lives. We know Martin Luther King Jr. really believed in nonviolence, not because he preached it, but because when punched in the mouth, he refused to retaliate. Our hearts were drawn to Rick and Kay Warren, when in the face of suffering over the suicide of their son, they publicly forgave the one who gave him the gun that took his life. The emblem of our faith is not the image of a pulpit Jesus preached from but the cross he suffered on. Jesus had been wronged, and at his disposal, he had legions of angels who at any given moment could have taken him down from the cross and slaughtered his accusers. Yet with all this power at his fingertips, he begged God to forgive his handlers and hecklers.

How we respond to those who wrong us is the clearest test of what we actually believe. Your convictions cannot be discerned in temperature-controlled environments, ivory towers, or church facilities. As my dad says, "We don't live in heaven and board down here." God saves us and washes us in his amazing grace while leaving us here on earth to display his incredible, performance-free love in the pantheon of evil and difficulty. Suffering and being wronged can become the stage on which the redemptive power of our faith is unleashed. There can be but one real test to know if you have truly been washed in God's performance-free love: How do I respond to others whose performance doesn't quite measure up with me?

Several years ago, a man named Charles Carl Roberts murdered five Amish girls and wounded five others. A God-fearing community in Nickels Mines, Pennsylvania, found itself reeling in the aftermath of this horrific act. We in the global village were aghast at his cowardice behavior (he committed suicide right after his killing spree). But we were also left wondering how these God followers would respond. Soon afterward, our questions were answered. Still reeling in their own woundedness, somehow the elders of the community mustered up the courage to go over to the home of Roberts's widow. They embraced her, gave her money to care for her children, and told her they forgave her. When one of these God fearers was asked why they forgave, he responded by saying they were Christians, and that's what Christians do. They forgive.

This is what it means to abide in God's love for us. God's anti-meritocracy love for us is not some touchy-feely, ethereal idea where struggle is nonexistent and we're left with an untested kind of faith. No. The reason God lavishes us with his love while leaving us in a world filled with evil, violence, and injustice is that his band of Jesus lovers can model this countercultural, performance-free love to the wonderment of the world and the glory of God. Isn't this Louie Zamperini's story, and the reason the book about his life (*Unbroken*) captivated millions of readers? Take suffering out of Louie Zamperini's narrative, and it's not worth hearing. Instead, what drew us to him was his refusal to be mastered by it—his relentless commitment to forgive his tormentors, especially the one called "The Bird." What both Louie and the Amish community in Pennsylvania pass on is a valuable lesson: We know we're abiding in God's amazing love when we strip our tormentors of their power over us by forgiving them over and over and over again.

And so it is with you and me. God doesn't want us to be reservoirs of his love, but rivers, where what we have received from him touches others. So when our fellow human siblings fail to perform—with every injustice done to us and every time we're gossiped about, lied about, swindled, and even abused—there stands an amazing opportunity to drench people with God's performance-free love called forgiveness.

FORGIVENESS IS NOT RECONCILIATION

This is Jesus' point as we come to Matthew 18. I find it interesting that Jesus uses the word *church* only two times in his ministry—both in the gospel of Matthew. The first time is in chapter 16, and the second comes two chapters later. Jesus' use of *church* in chapter 18 interests me because of his emphasis on relational trauma and forgiveness. Beginning in verse 15, Jesus unfolds a strategy on how to deal with someone who has wronged us. Where has this wrong taken place? In the church (verse 17). It's fair to assume the church will have its share of messiness since it is filled with people.

In verse 21, you can see Peter still chewing on what Jesus just said in verse 15, because he asks Jesus exactly how many times he could be wronged by his brother and yet still forgive him. Always eager to jump in, Peter offers an answer to his own question: "Up to seven times?" (NASB). He's got to be smiling when he says "seven times." The rabbis in Jesus' day taught you only had to forgive *three* times. Peter thinks he's going the extra mile when he takes the number three, doubles it, then adds one to land him on the number of completion. In his estimation, Peter is being generous.

Never to be outdone, Jesus wipes the smile off Peter's face when he says, "I do not say to you, up to seven times, but up to seventy times seven" (verse 22 NASB). Four hundred ninety is a long way from seven. And in case you're feeling relieved because there's someone in your life who is number 489, Jesus is employing hyperbole. He's exaggerating to make a point. It's like the frustrated parent who says to her child, "I've told you a million times to take out the trash." We know you haven't literally said it a million times, but you're overstating the case to make a point. This is what Jesus is doing here, and the point he's making is that our horizontal forgiveness is to know no limits, because the vertical forgiveness we have received from God knows no limits. To follow Jesus means heaping all-you-can-eat helpings of forgiveness onto the plates of our tormentors.

Some of you are saying, "Hmm, what about my wayward

spouse who continues to cheat on me or abuse me?" Or, "What about that belligerent 'friend' who shows no regard for me and continues to gossip about me and slander me?" Do I ignore the philandering spouse, suck it up, and stay, refusing to separate or divorce? Is there ever a point in which I stop trying to make amends with the so-called friend who shows no respect for me or our relationship? Is it ever okay to just move on?

What Jesus is communicating has everything to do with forgiveness—and not reconciliation. These are two very different concepts. Reconciliation has to do with the restoration of the relationship; forgiveness is the letting go of the offense, a refusal to be mastered by the wrong. While we can't reconcile without forgiving, we can forgive without reconciling. Reconciliation takes two; forgiveness requires one. Paul spoke of this in Romans 12: "If it is possible, as far as it depends on you, live at peace with everyone" (verse 18). Paul is concerned with reconciliation—the restoration of the relationship and the bringing together of people who were formerly at odds. Here, though, Paul gives a loophole when he says "if it is possible." Paul understands that reconciliation takes two, and that there are times when one party will do everything within their means to make the relationship work, but without mutual commitment, it just won't happen. Reconciliation is the ideal. God hates divorce and wants your marriage to work. He wants your friendship restored. But it takes two ferociously committed people to have a flourishing relationship. Forgiveness and reconciliation are not the same thing.

FORGIVENESS ON REPEAT

Jesus, though, offers no loopholes on forgiveness. "Seventy times seven" has to be the most difficult math problem in the world, but this is what it means to follow Jesus and display God's performance-free love. Right on the heels of his impossible equation, Jesus tells an illustration to clarify his point that forgiveness should have no expiration date.

There was a man who racked up a ton of debt—in the Greek, "ten thousand talents," to be exact (Matthew 18:24). One talent was worth years of wages, so ten thousand talents is a hopeless case. One commentator suggests this man owes millions of dollars; another says billions; and yet another scholar says he owes zillions. The point here is not the exact amount of his indebtedness, but his sheer hopelessness in paying it. What he owes is equivalent to putting America's ever-mounting debt on one person. Impossible.

So it should sound more than shocking that this man would say to his master, "Be patient with me . . . and I will pay back everything" (Matthew 18:26). *Really? Are you serious? And how long is that going to take?* His offer to pay his debt is as laughable as me thinking I can work my way into heaven by my own moral efforts. This is Jesus' point. In this parable, the master is God; we are the servants; and the debt represents our sins. It is as hopeless for us to get into a relationship with God on our own as it was for this man to pay off his debt.

Now if I were to be approached with this kind of offer, I think my anger would only spike. This servant is insulting his master's sensibilities. But instead of being offended or angered, the master does something even more surprising than the servant's offer. Without any negotiations, he not only refuses his offer but lets him go scot-free: "The servant's master took pity on him, canceled the debt, and let him go" (Matthew 18:27). God's grace and forgiveness are more amazing than our sins and offenses.

If you're looking for a good forgiveness definition, look

no further than Matthew 18:27: "The servant's master . . . let him go." Forgiveness is a letting go; it's a defiant refusal to be mastered by the hurt, anger, and bitterness of the offense. Forgiveness is not amnesia. It is not a macho shrugging of the shoulders and acting as if the offense never happened. No, the master knows how much this servant owed him, and this probably wasn't the first time he tried to collect on the money. Come on, one doesn't rack up this kind of debt without getting a few phone calls from bill collectors. Knowing full well the offense, the master lets it go.

FORGIVENESS IS IRRATIONAL

Forgiveness is really irrational, isn't it? What makes sense is to keep score and to get revenge. And so some of us lash out verbally, saying hurtful things, in our own little way trying to settle the score. Okay, maybe that's not exactly you. Some of us are way too sophisticated and "mature" to let people know they got to us. So we choose a more passive route—all of a sudden becoming too busy, not returning phone calls or texts, silently erecting walls, and drifting out of the relationship, all the while brooding over the offense. Whether you're like Al Green's ex-wife, who threw a hot pot of grits on him to settle the score, or more of the silent "assassin" type, who when offended can only say, "That's okay," while you plan your escape, either route is unforgiveness, a failure to let it go.

When I was in college, I got one of those anxiety-filled phone calls from my mother, letting me know my dad had just had a close brush with tragedy. Driving down a road, a man came flying through a stoplight and crashed into the passenger's side of my dad's car. Had the impact come on the driver's side, I would be writing about my deceased father.

When Dad emerged from his vehicle, still dazed by the deployed air bag and suddenness of the event, he was met with a barrage of racist epithets hurled from the elderly white driver of the car, who was completely at fault. My dad's first inclination was to lay hands on him—and not for the purpose of prayer, if you know what I mean. Thankfully, he restrained. Later that day, my dad found himself at lunch, weeping with a friend while wondering out loud why he was still thought of as some "nigger."

Hearing all this caused my blood to boil. I was beside myself as Dad relayed the story to me. I wanted to get on the next plane, find this man, and give it to him straight, if I can be honest. (Thankfully, God has grown me a lot in the several decades since the incident.) As our conversation was winding down, I'll never forget what my dad said to me: "Son, will you pray I get the chance to share the love of God with him, and that God will help me to forgive?"

I remember thinking my father has to be crazy. Could it be the accident caused some head trauma? Forgive this man who was clearly at fault and who called you some vile names, pillaging your dignity and seeking to devastate your humanity? Forgive? Now that's crazy, but I guess that's the whole point. There are a million reasons my dad should not have forgiven this man, and there are just as many reasons you shouldn't forgive the hurt inflicted on you. I've learned over the years that if forgiveness doesn't have a little crazy to it, it's probably not genuine forgiveness. Forgiveness, Jesus teaches, is irrational; what's rational is to keep score.

But it's exactly when we refuse to keep score by forgiving that we astound the world with our redemptive absurdity. To my knowledge, the man who violated my dad never responded to Dad's irrational act of forgiveness. Who knows, maybe in his own way he did. But if I were a betting man, I'd feel comfortable making a wager that at the very least, he was in awe of the performance-free love shown to him.

FORGIVENESS IS COSTLY

So this man owes ten thousand talents, and we get that his master has no hope of getting all of it back, but he can get some of it back, right? To just let the indebted servant go without recouping even part of the debt costs the master some money. There's literally a cost to his forgiveness.

Tim Keller points out that forgiveness is a suffering.[1] When you do something wrong to me, I want to respond by wronging you back. I want to inflict hurt on you. I well remember the time a couple in our church desperately needed help. The husband had offended the wife. To punish him, she withheld sex for well over a year. The time frame is a bit extreme, but her actions are somewhat understandable, humanly speaking. This is how sin has hard-wired us. Wrong me, and I'll get you back, doing all I can to inflict hurt on you.

It is what's called "the Chicago way." In the movie *The Untouchables*, Sean Connery's character advises Elliot Ness about how to bring down Al Capone and his gang. He knows a hornet's nest of violence is about to be stirred up. He says, "He pulls a knife; you pull a gun. He sends one of yours to the hospital; you send one of his to the morgue. *That's* the *Chicago way.*" And so it is with human relationships. You upset me; I end the relationship. You cheat on me; I cheat back. You go over the budget by fifty dollars; I go over by a hundred. That's the Chicago way.

The problem with this ethic is that it has a flawed understanding of humanity and leaves no margin for error. The

Chicago way does not even attempt to understand mercy and grace. The very nature of humanity is relational dysfunction—constant failings to perform and measure up to my expectations of you. Spend time with a person long enough, and they're bound to disappoint you. When your friend doesn't perform, when your spouse messes up the checkbook—again—and when your in-laws' idiosyncrasies prove too invasive, and you respond with the Chicago way, get ready for a life of loneliness, with a long trail of broken relationships. There's no way any of us will know the joy of long-term, sustained relationships without knowing the pain of forgiveness.

Forgiveness should hurt. Look at the pain Jesus endured on the cross while he exhaled the words, "Father, forgive them" (Luke 23:34). The reason we don't forgive is so we can inflict some sort of pain on the offender. When we refuse to go the Chicago way, however, we, through our forgiveness, inflict pain not on our offender but on our own ego-driven lust for vengeance.

Nelson Mandela spent years in captivity on Robben Island, all for fighting for the basic human rights of equality and dignity. Robben Island may be off the coast of Cape Town, South Africa, but it's certainly no day at the beach. While incarcerated, Mandela was ridiculed by his white jailers and forced to do dehumanizing things.

When Mandela later became president of South Africa, there was a lot of angst about what exactly the nation and world were getting. Many expected to see a man driven by vengeance, waiting to exact retribution. But these concerns were laid to rest on the eve of his inauguration, when Mandela surprised many by inviting as his honored guest one of the white jailers who had tormented him. This irrational, costly act of forgiveness had to cut against the grain of his humanity. For Mandela to let go of the years of ridicule inflicted suffering not on his offender but on the unpleasant part of all of us that seeks to be satisfied by vengeance. To forgive is costly. If it doesn't hurt, it's probably not forgiveness.

FORGIVENESS IS FREEING

Jesus' tale takes a turn, as this newly emancipated man immediately goes out and finds a person who owes him a few hundred denarii. Ignoring his debtor's pleas for mercy, the man begins to choke him, demanding payment. The irony of it all leaves us stunned. Here this man has just been forgiven something like America's debt, yet he refuses to set free the one who is indebted to him over what amounts to be, comparatively speaking, a few dollars? Incredible!

Taking in the scene are a few servants who belong to this hypocrite's former master. Aghast by what they've witnessed, they go back to their master and give him a full report. Enraged, the master reneges on his offer of freedom: "'You wicked servant! . . . I canceled all that debt of yours because you begged me to. Shouldn't you have had mercy on your fellow servant just as I had on you?' In anger his master handed him over to the jailers to be tortured, until he should pay back all he owed" (Matthew 18:32–34).

The servant's refusal to forgive lands *him* in a jail that offers no hope of freedom. Earlier, though, when he was forgiven, the jail was thrown open, and he was free. Forgiveness is the greatest gift, not that we give to others, but that we give to ourselves.

Some years ago, the cover of *Spirituality and Health* had a picture of three United States ex-soldiers in front of the Vietnam Memorial in Washington, D.C. One soldier asks, "Have you forgiven those who held you prisoner of war?" Another soldier replies, "I will never forgive them." "Then it seems they still have you in prison, don't they?" responds his mate.[2]

It's counterintuitive, isn't it? Someone hurts us—I mean, really knocks the wind out of us, and our reflex reaction is to go the Chicago way—tit for tat. Why do we do this? We want to inflict hurt and pain on our abusers. We think our "little acts" of unforgiveness will hurt them. But we're surprised when we discover, some time later, that our refusal to forgive didn't so much hurt them as it hurt us.

When I was called "nigger" by one of my classmates in college, it sent me on a downward spiral that lasted more than a decade. Over time, I not only found myself hating white people, but I also discovered a loss of joy, which was replaced by negativity and cynicism. Technically, I didn't discover these things; I had them pointed out by some of my close friends, who watched me devolve deeper and deeper into bitterness. It didn't take me long to figure out the culprit. I had allowed one man's actions, and my refusal to forgive, to have a personality-altering power over my life that no one was meant to have but God alone. And you know what's crazy about it all? Here I am, ten years later, spending a lot of time thinking about and being upset with a man who in all likelihood was no longer even thinking about me. His actions hadn't changed me; my failure to forgive him did. When we refuse to forgive, we think we're hurting others, but the only one we really hurt is ourselves. It's crazy, but when you and I refuse to forgive, we, like this servant, are not free; we end up in jail—held captive by our own unforgiveness.

WHY FORGIVE?

The times I've been most assured I'm abiding in God's love is when I've been cut the deepest by others, and yet somehow I've been able to eke out the words, "I forgive you." I sincerely believe the mountaintop of the Christian life is found on the other side of the valley of hurt, when we trust God to take us to the peak of forgiveness.

The older I get, the more I find myself valuing people and being real slow to let friendships go. What this demands is a steady cultivating of relationships, tending to the weeds always poised to sabotage a friendship. If you don't have time to give yourself fully to the few God will send your way, don't complain about loneliness. Friendship is work, and one of the necessary essentials to a healthy union is forgiveness.

When I'm wronged by another and the silent assassin in me stands ready to end the relationship, what beckons me to roll up my sleeves and do the work of forgiveness is the cross and the reminder of my daily assaults on God. I need to hear, "Hey, you were the one who owed ten thousand talents, a debt you could never repay, but God did something crazy. He let it go." So for me to pitch a fit over an act of gossip or a moral failure is as ridiculous as this man going out and finding a debtor who owed him a few bucks, choking him, and demanding payment, all the while forgetting he was just forgiven a debt he could never repay. Unforgiveness is one of the highest forms of hypocrisy for the "Christian."

I put the word *Christian* in quotes because of how Jesus ends our story. This unforgiving servant is now thrown back in jail. The story ends with, "This is how my heavenly Father will treat each of you unless you forgive your brother or sister from your heart" (Matthew 18:35). Scary words, right? Jesus is questioning the validity of our salvation. I mean, can I really say I'm in relationship with God, having received his forgiveness, and then withhold that same forgiveness from others? If you're looking for a reason to forgive the woman who cheated on you and split up your home, then look to the cross as you write the next child support payment.

This sounds impossible, and it should. Notice Jesus does not end the story by saying "unless you forgive with your mouth," but "unless you forgive from your heart." Now I can somewhat control my mouth and *say* I forgive while not meaning it. Children are a great example of this. But what I cannot control are the meditations of my heart, and this is where I need God to work. Authentic forgiveness—not a gold-plated forgiveness but a solid-gold kind of forgiveness—can only happen by the work of God. Jesus understood this. He taught us to pray, "Forgive us our sins, for we also forgive everyone who sins against us" (Luke 11:4). Begging God to forgive me reminds me of my need to forgive others.

The Lord's Prayer is a daily prayer, and this helps me when it comes to forgiveness. I don't know about you, but some offenses run so deep that one prayer won't do. I need to daily ask God to do a work of grace that reaches beyond my mouth and into my heart.

But there's another reason we should forgive—a reason modeled well in recent years by our South African brothers and sisters. *No Future Without Forgiveness* is Bishop Desmond Tutu's history of a government-sanctioned committee whose sole purpose was to bring about forgiveness (and reconciliation)—The Truth and Reconciliation Commission. It would not be a stretch to say what kept South Africa from venturing down the same path of implosion as Northern Island or Kosovo was the TRC and its insistence on collective memory and communal forgiveness as a means of experiencing *ubuntu*.

In America's individualized culture, *ubuntu* is almost impossible to translate because of the communal nature of the word. Reaching for words to convey the term, Tutu explains *ubuntu* this way: "It is to say, 'My humanity is caught up, is inextricably bound up, in yours.' We belong in a bundle of life.

We say, 'A person is a person through other persons.' It is not, 'I think therefore I am.' It says rather: 'I am human because I belong.'"[3]

Bishop Tutu unearths the philosophical and theological underpinnings of the TRC. Their relentless commitment to not just forget the atrocities of apartheid and move forward as if nothing happened, but to remember and to present the offender to the offended was based on *ubuntu*—the notion that I am incomplete without you—even my offender. If we carry *ubuntu* to its extreme, we are left with the idea that a failure to forgive actually dehumanizes the offended in the same way that the offender, through his offenses, acted in a less than fully human way.

Bishop Tutu tells of a case where a group of police officers shot a black man in the back of the head, watched the body convulse to its death, and then, to cover the offense, roasted the body in a fire for seven hours. As the body slowly began to decompose, these police officers poured drinks and started a barbecue to the side, enjoying their food and drink.[4] If there's a definition of inhumanity, this is it. In a separate case, one victim recalled the time he was tortured, thinking of his tormentors, "By the way, these are God's children and yet they are behaving like animals. They need us to help them recover the humanity they have lost."[5] Bishop Tutu argues well: The way we give back our oppressors their humanity is by forgiving. Why? He writes:

> We are bound up in a delicate network of interdependence because, as we say in our African idiom, a person is a person through other persons. To dehumanize another inexorably means that one is dehumanized as well. It is not too surprising that, having been involved in a policy as evil and dehumanizing as apartheid, cabinet minister Jimmy

Kruger could heartlessly declare that the death in detention of a Steve Biko "left him cold." Thus to forgive is indeed the best form of self-interest since anger, resentment, and revenge are corrosive of that *summum bonum*, that greatest good, communal harmony that enhances the humanity and personhood of all in the community.[6]

Forgiving those who wrong us restores not only their humanity but ours as well. When we forgive, we refuse to become less than human and choose instead to be fully human. Think of the civil rights movement. It took full humanity for those in my parents' generation to not return evil for evil and to let it go.

Looking to the same cross that Dr. Martin Luther King Jr. and his army gazed on, we find *ubuntu* in its purest form. Jesus' "Father, forgive them" was not only an intercessory plea for salvation but also an act of restoring back to their humanity those who had lied, spit on, and mocked him.

The years I spent refusing to forgive my college classmate and wallowing in suspicion over my white siblings revealed my flawed anthropology. It is arrogant to dismiss a whole race of people as unnecessary, just as it is arrogant to act in racist ways as if your race is superior. We need one another. The offended needs the offender. The gossip needs the one gossiped about, just as the one gossiped about needs the gossip. To erect a wall, ignore the person, and treat them as if they never existed is to disown the very one Christ died for and stands ready to offer his performance-free love to. The unforgiving "Christian" puts on a display of arrogance, assuming in their unforgiveness that they are the only ones truly worthy of being forgiven, of receiving God's performance-free love.

Please don't hear me as downplaying the betrayal or the hurt. The neighbor or sick family member who crawled into bed and abused you should be prosecuted. Justice and forgiveness can comingle. God is both just and forgiving. Reconciliation may be completely out of the question, and rightly so. But the "beast" Desmond Tutu talks about—that person who wronged you—needs to be looked in the eye and forgiven.[7] Or could it be that forgiveness becomes the kiss that turns beasts into princes. Fully human. *Ubuntu.*

CHAPTER 10

the indicator light
of the kingdom

PRACTICING GENEROSITY

Justice is what love looks like in public.
Cornel West

My understanding of what it means to love and follow God was shaped in the independent Baptist church I attended during my formative years. These were dear people who loved God sincerely. Whatever good God has done with my life, I owe a ton to that church and its people. As is true in any community, some things they aced, and others they failed at.

Most of what I learned from my church about Jesus wasn't spoken, just implied. If you were to ask me what it meant to be righteous when I was, say, fifteen, I probably would have told you the righteous person came to church every Sunday morning and Sunday evening—oh, and Wednesday night too. If I had thought a little more about your question, I would have said the righteous person didn't have sex outside of marriage and served in some ministry—like being on the usher board. They won the sword drill competitions at vacation Bible school and caravanned to our summer camp in Tennessee every summer as well. Oh, and the righteous person, at least as far as my fifteen-year-old mind could tell, gave every month to the building fund too (though when I left for college, they hadn't even come close to beginning construction—but that's another tale altogether).

Jesus' sermon in Matthew 25, though, gives a different angle into the face of the righteous person. Sure, coming to church, serving in ministry, and even giving to the building fund are aspects of what it means to be righteous, but according to Jesus, there's more.

When it comes to money and possessions, our culture says it's nobody's business but yours. But this is not the way of Jesus. In perhaps his most "un-American" sermon, Jesus says some pretty scary things in Matthew 25:31–46. Moments away from his betrayal, death, and resurrection, Jesus' piercing words go against the grain of the American Dream of personal aggrandizement and comfort:

> "When the Son of Man comes in his glory, and all the angels with him, he will sit on his glorious throne. All the nations will be gathered before him, and he will separate the people one from another as a shepherd separates the sheep from the goats. He will put the sheep on his right and the goats on his left.
>
> "Then the King will say to those on his right, 'Come, you who are blessed by my Father; take your inheritance, the kingdom prepared for you since the creation of the world. For I was hungry and you gave me something to eat, I was thirsty and you gave me something to drink, I was a stranger and you invited me in, I needed clothes and you clothed me, I was sick and you looked after me, I was in prison and you came to visit me.'
>
> "Then the righteous will answer him, 'Lord, when did we see you hungry and feed you, or thirsty and give you something to drink? When did we see you a stranger and

invite you in, or needing clothes and clothe you? When did we see you sick or in prison and go to visit you?'

"The King will reply, 'Truly I tell you, whatever you did for one of the least of these brothers and sisters of mine, you did for me.'

"Then he will say to those on his left, 'Depart from me, you who are cursed, into the eternal fire prepared for the devil and his angels. For I was hungry and you gave me nothing to eat, I was thirsty and you gave me nothing to drink, I was a stranger and you did not invite me in, I needed clothes and you did not clothe me, I was sick and in prison and you did not look after me.'

"They also will answer, 'Lord, when did we see you hungry or thirsty or a stranger or needing clothes or sick or in prison, and did not help you?'

"He will reply, 'Truly I tell you, whatever you did not do for one of the least of these, you did not do for me.'

"Then they will go away to eternal punishment, but the righteous to eternal life.'"

Matthew 25:31–46

Giving our lives away to the least of these—the incarcerated, infirm, and hungry—this is how Jesus understands the righteous. I remember when I first came to terms with this passage some years ago. Jesus' words shook me to the core, because he seems to suggest that if I am not disadvantaging myself for the advantage of others as a regular way of life, I may not be a genuine follower of him. Ouch—and what if this is true?

Feeding the hungry, visiting the imprisoned, serving the poor and the sick—are these not works that lead the way to eternal life? *Wait a minute*, I know you're thinking. *This sounds like performance faith!* Not so fast. God's performance-free love does require us to take action, but it's *how* we respond to that action that makes all the difference.

TRACING THE STORY OF GRACE

Now we seem to have a problem, don't we? Jesus begins by saying we must regularly give our lives away to the least of these—the infirmed, incarcerated, sick, naked, homeless—and if we don't, we'll be counted among the goats who will spend an eternity separated from him.

Jesus' words here are troubling. I mean, just reading our text, it's easy to walk away thinking that what gets you and me into the kingdom is what we do for the poor—and this sounds like a works-oriented, performance-driven salvation, doesn't it? So give the homeless woman some money, and if you do enough of this, then you've earned an eternity in heaven. If this is true, then I've just blown my whole argument in this book, making it okay for us to continue trying to white-knuckle our way into the kingdom of God.

But the Bible—from Genesis to Revelation—says we don't have to do anything other than trust in God's gracious gift of salvation by faith, and we will be saved. So what's really going on here?

I used to teach a course on how to study the Bible—a topic called hermeneutics. One of the geeky jokes my colleagues and I used to crack is when it comes to Bible interpretation, the three laws are "context, context, context." Not funny, I know, but there's some truth here. If we look at the whole context of Scripture, we discover—from Genesis to Revelation—a consistent theme: We are saved by grace through faith, and not by our own efforts.

For example, I could take you to Genesis 15:6, which states,

"Abram believed the LORD, and he credited it to him as righteousness." The writers of the New Testament understood this to be the moment when Abraham (formerly known as Abram) entered into relationship with God (see Romans 4:3, e.g.). What's interesting is that Genesis 15 tells of Abram getting saved, but two chapters later, he is circumcised, which means that even under the old covenant, faith precedes works. What encourages me is we later find Abraham lying on several occasions, but God keeps walking in relationship with his son. Everything about Abraham shows salvation is about grace, not about earning God's favor.

In the book of Exodus, we see God delivering the people of Israel from the Egyptians in an astounding succession of ten plagues. God tells his people that if they want to get out of the final plague unscathed, they have to put the blood of a spotless lamb over the sides and tops of the doorframes of their homes, and the death angel will pass over their houses—this is where we get the word *Passover*. God's people weren't spared by giving more money, finding a poor person to befriend, or refraining from certain acts. No. What spared them was showing their faith in God by finding a spotless lamb, killing it, and placing its blood on their doorframes (Exodus 12:7). Do you see the connection to what God and his Son, Jesus, have done for us? This Old Testament picture makes a great new-covenant point: What saves us isn't our human efforts, but our faith in God—by accepting the blood of his spotless Lamb, Jesus, as the only cure to cleanse us from our sins.

When we get to the New Testament, the writers don't so much paint pictures of this truth as make powerful statements, all attesting to the fact that we are saved by grace through faith:

Therefore, since we have been justified through faith, we have peace with God through our Lord Jesus Christ.

Romans 5:1

For it is by grace you have been saved, through faith— and this is not from yourselves, it is the gift of God—not by works, so that no one can boast.

Ephesians 2:8–9

Talk about good news! I can't get to God's astounding love on my own. I need his amazing, gracious gift of his only Son, Jesus Christ.

YOUR SPIRITUAL "CHECK ENGINE SOON" LIGHT

Your car has a dashboard with all kinds of gauges and indicator lights. One tells you how much gas you have; another alerts you to the temperature of your engine—and then there are a series of lights that indicate potential problems with your vehicle. These gauges and lights tell us what's really going on underneath the hood of our cars. While we may hate to see the "check engine soon" light, we're grateful for it because it lets us know what's really going on.

Money and possessions are indicator lights that alert us to the true condition of our hearts. We never like to talk about them because it makes us feel emotionally naked and vulnerable. In Matthew 25:31–46, Jesus isn't disagreeing with what the Bible teaches—just the opposite. His sermon has nothing to do with how we get into the kingdom, but everything to do with how we can tell the kingdom is in us. When Korie and I respond to God's grace by giving generously to the poor, it's an indicator light to show we're really experiencing God's performance-free love.

If we're *not* doing anything for the least of these brothers and sisters of ours, if we're not rolling up our sleeves and engaging in defending the oppressed or advocating for justice, this could be an indicator light to check under the hood and peer into our hearts. What I do with money doesn't make me a child of God; it just shows me if I really am. See the difference?

WESLEY AND WHEAT FIELDS

John Wesley was the founder of the Methodist Church, and a great preacher used by God to bring about global transformation. But before he was any of that, Wesley was a student at Oxford University who was concerned about the indicator light of money. So one year, he asked himself a hard question: "How much money do I need to live on for this year?" He ran some numbers and concluded that twenty-eight pounds was all he needed. Anything more he would give to the poor. That first year, he made thirty pounds. True to his word, he lived off the twenty-eight and gave away the other two. Wesley thought to himself, *I've stumbled on to something. I think I'll do this for the rest of my life.* Even when his income reached above a thousand pounds, he continued to live off only twenty-eight and gave away the rest.[1]

John Wesley asked himself a question I haven't heard too many people in the twenty-first century consider: *How much is enough?* How much is enough house? How much is enough clothes? Shoes? Cars? Purses? How much, really, is enough?

It's hard to hear this story about John Wesley and not have your mind wander to this passage in the book of Leviticus:

> When you reap the harvest of your land, do not reap to the very edges of your field or gather the gleanings of your

harvest. Do not go over your vineyard a second time or pick up the grapes that have fallen. Leave them for the poor and the foreigner. I am the LORD your God.

Leviticus 19:9–10.

To the farming community of the Israelites, land was what money is to most of us today. Now I don't have a degree in farming—if such a thing exists—but I do know that not gathering all the gleanings of your harvest is to literally leave money on the table. So when I try to hear Leviticus 19 with my farmer hat on, I've got a dilemma. God seems to be asking me to give up some money by not gathering all the gleanings of my food so the poor and the person passing through can have something to eat. This not only insults my capitalist sensibilities; it cuts against the grain of my fallen heart.

If, like me, you're not a farmer, you're probably asking how in the world Leviticus 19 applies to you. Well, it does. When I consider this text from my New York City apartment, I believe God is telling me that when I look at my budget (which is the equivalent of my field), don't max it out. Instead, I should leave some margin to spontaneously and generously give to the poor. Think about it: There's just no way Matthew 25 happens unless I navigate my finances with Leviticus 19 principles in mind. God wants us to leave room to spontaneously and generously give to the poor and the hurting.

I imagine you could be feeling some shame right now when you think about money and what God wants you to do with it. I've been there—sure I have. Who hasn't gone through seasons of selfishness and apathy when it comes to the least of these?

So feeling the weight of Jesus' sermon, you feel obligated to write a check or take a homeless person to lunch. Let me stop you right there. Shame is an awful change agent. Lasting change never comes in the lap of shame, but only when we're inspired—and nothing inspires more than grace.

If the regular rhythms of our lives are going to be with the least of these, then we must see our labors no longer in the category of the *have to* but the *get to*. If you want to move from duty to delight, I have found it helpful to spend time considering the generosity of Jesus toward me and allow it to inspire my generosity toward others: "You know the grace of our Lord Jesus Christ, that though he was rich, yet for your sake he became poor, so that you through his poverty might become rich" (2 Corinthians 8:9). The writer, Paul, talks about Jesus being rich. As God's Son, Jesus was rich, enjoying the comforts of heaven. But someone had to come to suffer and die so we could be saved. So what does Jesus do? He steps out of the comfort of heaven, takes on human flesh, and suffers the ridicule, belittlement, and horror of the cross. Why? So we could receive an inheritance and live fully immersed in God's performance-free love. Now at any given point, Jesus could have said, "I like it in heaven. I don't want to go to earth. Let them suffer and die for their own sins. They got themselves into all of this." But he didn't. Paul says Jesus embraced poverty so we could be rich. You and I are saved by the generosity of Jesus. Want to be inspired to live a generous life? Consider how spiritually destitute you were before Jesus. Contemplate his generosity, and allow that to motivate your generosity toward others. Now we're moving from *have to* to *get to*.

INSPIRED GENEROSITY

It's just a truism in life: Nothing inspires generosity more than when we have experienced generosity from others. I've seen this in my own life. There was no way I could afford seminary—just no way. I had a desire to go; I just didn't have the means to pay. No problem. My seminary took care of that when I got awarded a scholarship. I remember driving down the 105 freeway in Los Angeles, my cheeks soaked with tears, thanking God after I got a letter telling me my schooling was paid for. Now let me ask you a question: Do you think I've written a few checks to their alumni fund since my graduation? You bet I have. Are these checks duty or delight? They're sheer delight. Having received generosity, how can I not be generous in return?

The older I get, the more I'm convinced God has arranged things in such a way that you and I become the primary means by which people are cared for and loved. This isn't about some government program or agenda. In fact, if the body of Christ is ready to respond to Jesus' generosity to us, there's enough money in the church of America to feed, clothe, and empower the poor.[2] God has given you a field. It may not be as big as someone else's, but in all likelihood, you have one. Don't glean to the edges. Leave some room for the sick, imprisoned, hungry, and oppressed. When you do this as a response to God's amazing love for you, not as an effort to obtain his love, it's an indicator light revealing that you are truly a part of his kingdom.

CHAPTER 11

God's got you

PRACTICING PEACE OVER WORRY

*The lesson of life is that somehow we have been
enabled to bear the unbearable and to do the undoable
and to pass the breaking point and not to break.
The lesson of life is that worry is unnecessary.*
William Barclay

*"Can any one of you by worrying add
a single hour to your life?"*
Jesus, in Matthew 6:27

I used to believe if I only had more, I would worry less. Made sense, until I stumbled upon a biography of Howard Hughes, the billionaire, film pioneer, and aviator who spent decades as a frightened recluse cowering in the darkness of a cordoned-off hotel room. Hughes was so convinced someone was out to get him or some germ would wipe him out that he refused to allow anyone to see him for long stretches of time. As you can imagine, this posed a bit of a challenge when it came to running a business. So when the time came to get Hughes's attention on some important matter, specific directives were given about how to communicate with him. There was no barging into his room. Oh no. You would need to take several tissues, and while covering the doorknob with them, you would knock and open the door ever so slightly, lest you would spread contagion. One time, an aide carried out these instructions but couldn't find Howard. Concerned, the aide broke protocol and looked inside the room, only to find that Howard was in the bathroom—a place he would spend the next twenty-seven hours.

On the very rare occasion Hughes ventured out, his driver would be directed to never exceed thirty-five miles an hour. If by chance they had to cross railroad tracks or an uneven part of the road, the driver was to slow down to two miles an hour. Howard was that nervous he'd get into a wreck.

Talk about a poster child for worry.

Billionaire Howard Hughes is a study in contrasts, an enigma wrapped in a riddle, illustrating an important timeless truth: Money and possessions do not inoculate us from worry; actually they heighten its likelihood.

Jesus preached about worry. In Matthew 6:25–33, he repeatedly cautions us against being anxious. Just before Jesus shares his thoughts about worry, he talks about the hopelessness of a life spent in pursuit of money (Matthew 6:19–24). It's impossible, Jesus cautions, to serve both God and money. Isn't it interesting that Jesus leaps from money and possessions to worry? I think there's something to this. Jesus is dismantling the notion that the more one has, the less worried they'll be.

WORRY'S MYTH

When Korie and I first got married, we moved into a little house in a tiny Southern California community. *Tiny*—now that's a fitting word not just for our town but for our home as well. Our "master bedroom" was so small that I had to move my dresser into the guest bedroom, and if Korie wasn't careful when she woke up in the morning, she could roll right into our closet. We didn't have much money, so date nights consisted of long walks into town, where we shared a snow cone and a cup of hot chocolate—and even then, money tended to be so tight that we could only go out once or twice a month.

Things have changed. No, we're not rich, but we can afford some of life's amenities, like vacations. Since those Sierra Madre days, we've bought a couple of houses and a few cars and have been able to give generously. God's been good. But there have been plenty of times when Korie and I reflected on those snow cone date nights with a glimmer in our eyes. Those moments had a simplicity and tranquility to them we now hunger for. Sure, we've taken on more salary, influence, and space—that is, until we moved to our apartment in New York City!—but with them, we've also accrued more stress and a larger capacity for worry.

We've got three kids now. As one of my friends is prone to say, "Children are like dangling your heart in front of you." I find myself worrying about my kids—there, I said it. I've worried about their health, grades, walk with Christ, and futures. What will become of them? I worry about my girl, Korie. I freaked out once when we found a lump in her neck, and then later a lump on her breast.

And speaking of freaking out, I once turned red—which for a black man is hard to do—about seven thousand feet in the air when one of the airplane's engines went out. I'm given to bouts of worry about the health and growth of our church and the quality of my sermons. It's said that Charles Spurgeon, the great London preacher, would sulk by the fire on Sunday afternoons if he wasn't pleased with the morning's sermon. Yeah, I've been there and done that—got the T-shirt and the hat. The more God has entrusted to me, the more vulnerable I am to worry.

So let's just put all the cards on the table. You'll never get to a point in life where you think you'll have everything you need externally to safeguard you from the internal disequilibrium called worry. As a single person, you're worried about always being single—so marriage will cure that, you think. Yeah, okay. You know how many couples worry about their spouse and the state of their marriage? Or you're married, and maybe you think having children will give you the satisfaction you've been searching for while also providing you with peace. Like Korie and me, you'll just be tempted to more worry as your heart is dangled in front of you. And speaking of children, I used to think once we got our kids out of the house, the worry would be over—or at least severely diminished. That changed when I saw the worry in my parents' faces over the health crisis we went through with one of our kids—their grandson. There is nothing in this life that will give you long-term calm and peace. Kids won't do it; neither will money or possessions.

THE PROBLEM WITH WORRY

Like a diamond resting on a piece of black velvet, the sheer beauty of God's performance-free love is only illumined when set against the background of struggle. We would have no clue what peace is unless everything around us said we should worry. The brilliance of God's glory can only be maximized when the waves of life and all of its problems come crashing against the home of our hearts. One of the ways we know we're resting in God's amazing love is when we refuse to give in to worry.

Jesus taught this. In an extensive excursus during his Sermon on the Mount, Jesus tells us three times not to worry:

> "Therefore I tell you, *do not worry* about your life, what you will eat or drink; or about your body, what you will wear. Is not life more than food, and the body more than clothes? . . . So *do not worry*, saying, 'What shall we eat?'

or 'What shall we drink?' or 'What shall we wear?' . . .
Therefore *do not worry* about tomorrow, for tomorrow will
worry about itself. Each day has enough trouble of its own."

Matthew 6:25, 31, 34, emphasis mine

Each "do not worry" is actually a command. Jesus, again, is
not suggesting something to try or giving us some sage wisdom
to contemplate. In fact, his use of command language means
worry is a sin. But why?

In verse 32, Jesus says, "For the pagans run after all these
things, and your heavenly Father knows that you need them."
Jesus is using the word *pagans* to picture people who aren't in
relationship with God—worldly people. Jesus is saying that
those who aren't in relationship with God are so distracted by
earthly items that they aren't focused on what really matters—
the eternal. So, Jesus argues, their eternal ADD actually serves
to heighten their sense of worry. When earth becomes our
obsession, anxiety becomes our lord. Worry is a warning sign
that cautions us about who our master really is. When I worry,
I join the company of worldly people who pledge allegiance to
the tyranny of things.

If I'm hearing Jesus right, he's saying, "Listen to me! I want
you to get this. When your lives are dominated by obsessing
over jobs, health, money, mortgage loans, the schools your kids
will attend, the clothes you'll wear, and the cars you'll drive, you
are acting like the world." When my life is overrun with worry,
I am revealing that my ultimate hope is not in a loving, caring
Father but in the things, people, and possessions of this world.

But there's another problem with worry. Jesus points it out
in verse 27: "Can any one of you by worrying add a single hour
to your life?" Worry, according to Jesus, is not only worldly;
it's useless.

The medical industry can drive us crazy, can't they? (Sorry, doctors, nurses, etc.!) When we found lumps on my wife's body and she underwent tests, we had to wait days to find out whether it was nothing or potentially life threatening. During the wait, I had to remind myself that worry was not going to change the diagnosis. Not one bit. Worry hasn't made one person pregnant or not pregnant. Worry won't protect the teenager who is out past curfew. Worry won't get you a job, a home, or a car loan. In fact, the only thing worry has proven to do is to negatively affect the worrier's health. Worry, Jesus says, is *useless*.

Remember my mention of C. S. Lewis in chapter 4 and his contention that all sin leads back to pride? Well, if worry is sinful, then it's just another face of pride. Jesus points this out when he says, "Therefore I tell you, do not worry about *your* life, what *you* will eat or drink; or about *your* body, what *you* will wear. Is not life more than food, and the body more than clothes" (Matthew 6:25, emphasis mine)? Do you see the personal pronouns here? What has mastered the worrier is a complete obsession with her life. She has contracted a myopia of sorts in which she can't see past her own world. Worry is a particular brand of narcissism worn by people who love to be in control—people like you and me. So when things have gotten a bit out of control for us, we obsess over how we can get back into control. We call this whole frantic search for control *worry*.

BEATING THE WORRY TRAP

Conquering worry is not some bucket-list item we check off, like climbing Mount Everest. It's more like cutting the grass, tending a garden, or making our bed—a task we return to continually. The Greeks offered a cure for overcoming worry. Certain Greeks held up the Stoics as a model of maturity, showing us the pathway to peace. It was the Stoics who threw up their hands and passively resigned themselves to the cards life had dealt them. Stuff your emotions and blindly accept your situation— that was their way of thinking. But this is not the way of Jesus:

> "Look at the birds of the air; they do not sow or reap or store away in barns, and yet your heavenly Father feeds them. Are you not much more valuable than they? Can any one of you by worrying add a single hour to your life?
>
> "And why do you worry about clothes? See how the flowers of the field grow. They do not labor or spin. Yet I tell you that not even Solomon in all his splendor was dressed like one of these. If that is how God clothes the grass of the field, which is here today and tomorrow is thrown into the fire, will he not much more clothe you—you of little faith?"
>
> *Matthew 6:26–30*

In his sermon, Jesus employs a rhetorical device known as an *a fortiori* argument—an argument from lesser to greater. Jesus starts out with animals (lesser) and ends with us humans (the greater). He begins by pointing to the birds of the air. They don't have a huge warehouse where they store worms in bulk. Birds don't have pantries or a second freezer in their garages to store more food. No, they take what they need for the day, living from one day to the next with no sense of worry about their food. God takes care of them.

Then Jesus diverts our attention from birds to flowers— flowers that Jesus tells us don't "labor or spin," and yet they are more glorious than the richest king ever—King Solomon. How does this happen? They're rooted in rich soil and receive rain and warm sunshine, all provided by a loving, gracious God without a single concern on their part.

Now, if God can take care of birds that live from day to day and flowers that exist in complete confidence in God's provision, how much more will God take care of us, who are made in his image and of more value than birds and flowers? As the psalmist says of humanity, "You have made them a little lower than the angels and crowned them with glory and honor. You made them rulers over the works of your hands; you put everything under their feet" (Psalm 8:5–6).

You know what God is saying here? You matter to him. He not only knows about your situation, but he also cares. God not only knows about your financial pressures but actually cares. He's not surprised by the tumor; he cares. It's worth repeating: God. Cares. So when you find yourself starting to tense up over sudden and unexpected news, remember that our pathway to a transcendent calm and an otherworldly peace is to feast on the truth of God's care.

There's something else. Jesus refers to God as our Father. What a perfect image to look to during stressful moments. God is our Papa, and we are his children. If there's one thing children can teach us (among many), it's that they are not prone to worry—at all. Sure, part of the reason is our kids can be clueless as to what's going on behind the scenes. But it's not like we are privy to any "insider trading" as to what God is doing with us. John Piper once quipped that at any given moment, God is up to ten thousand things in our lives, and we may be aware of three of them.[1]

When my oldest was about eight, I remember coming home from work and seeing him on our sofa—legs crossed, cookies in one hand and a remote in the other—watching TV. A few feet away, I embraced his mother and began to share with her what happened during my day. I guess we were too loud, because the next thing I knew, our son had paused his episode of *The*

Suite Life of Zack and Cody and asked us to keep it down. Talk about "first-world problems." All I could do was chuckle over the image. Here's my son not giving one thought about how the mortgage was going to get paid, where the money was going to come from to pay the cable bill, or how we'd keep his supply of cookies well stocked. Quentin just assumed he would be provided for. He may not say this to himself consciously, but it's the big assumption of his life: "Dad's got me."

God's got you. He really does. This is not some prosperity mumbo jumbo; it's biblical truth. You're going to get to the other side, because a loving, caring Father is holding your hand.

But what about all the Christ followers who faced stressful situations and were martyred for their faith or died of cancer, believing God would see them through? *How can you say, "God's got you," Bryan, when the law of averages tells us everyone will eventually die, and their very death, more times than not, will be a circumstance tempting them to worry? How can you say with confidence, "God's got you"?*

These are great questions—questions the apostle Paul can help with. Listen to what he writes to the Philippians: "I eagerly expect and hope that I will in no way be ashamed, but will have sufficient courage so that now as always Christ will be exalted in my body, whether by life or by death. For to me, to live is Christ and to die is gain" (Philippians 1:20–21).

Paul is in jail when he writes these words, not knowing what will become of him. Think about it. At any given moment, a government official could barge into his cell and drag him to his death. Talk about being tempted to worry. What's more, Paul says he doesn't know how the situation will turn out—"whether by life or by death." He has no control over his circumstances, but what he does know is this: Either way, Christ will be exalted. How can he speak with such a rich confidence? Paul knew this life is not all there is. Why would he say, "To die is gain"? What does he gain? Eternity with his Father. There's a tranquility in Paul's words, a confident peace, because he is convinced God has him, even if he were to die.

Dietrich Bonhoeffer was a German pastor who loved Jesus. Like Paul, he spent considerable time in prison, where he was ultimately executed. On a spring day in 1945, Bonhoeffer was taken to the gallows. His last words were, "This is the end—for me the beginning of life."[2] Where did such an otherworldly calm come from? Simply this: He knew that even in death, God's got him.

That's just how deep God's performance-free love goes.

Tense situations, especially life-threatening ones, scorch the soul's dross and unveil what we really believe about eternity. Worry is really a flawed eschatology. When I am consumed by worry, I'm saying this world is all there really is.

So something pops up out of life's left field, catching us off guard and leaving us with a feeling of emotional vertigo. How do we make it through? We remind ourselves God not only knows but also cares, and we trust our Father. And I've found another source of help in overcoming the temptation of worry: remembering God's provision.

When my parents were first married, they were still in college and money was so tight that splitting a snow cone and a cup of hot chocolate was completely out of the question. But then they got an unexpected bill, which meant they had only about fifty cents to live on until the next paycheck, which was more than a week away. When my dad got the news, he grabbed Mom's hand, and they got down on their knees and entrusted themselves to their caring heavenly Father, not knowing how they were going to make it. On a break between classes a few days later, Dad checked his mailbox and found an envelope from an organization for which he had spoken months before. They had been so late paying Dad that he had forgotten about it, but on this day, tucked inside the envelope were several hundred dollars. Their faithful Father had seen them through.

I wasn't around to see that episode of God's faithfulness, but I did see several others. Dad and Mom served for years at a nonprofit Christian organization where they had to raise their own salary from the generous gifts of others. Sometimes donations fell off and funds ran low, and then Dad would call us to pray around the dinner table, much the same way he and Mom had prayed in their tiny bedroom years before. Not once did I see Dad stressed out or overcome with worry, like Howard Hughes had been. Instead, I saw a dad who, with calm assurance, entrusted himself to his Dad in the full knowledge that God's got him. What peacefully navigated my parents through so many tense situations was knowing that God had delivered before, and he could do it again.

I wear the residue of their incredible calm in the face of tense moments. No, I don't bat a thousand in the peace department, but there have been plenty of times I've gone through the valley of worry with an incomprehensible tranquility, nourished by the memory of God's past faithfulness to my parents and me.

Ever since an airplane engine went out seven thousand feet in the air, I get a little nervous when turbulence comes my way. If you've flown, you know what turbulence is. It's an unsettling feeling, reminding you of how little control you actually have. You know what helps me deal with worry thousands of feet in the air? I look at the flight attendants. If they're still serving peanuts, pretzels, and drinks with smiles on their faces, I'm good. Their peace in the midst of uncertainty rubs off on me. It gives me a sense of serenity, even though I'm not exactly sure how things will turn out.

Several times in the gospels, we find Jesus sleeping in the midst of turbulence while his disciples are completely undone, fretting for their lives. Like a flight attendant serving Biscoff cookies while the plane is shaking, Jesus' serenity in turbulent times should have infused his followers with peace. No, Jesus' sleep doesn't mean he's unconcerned. Instead his sleep says, "I got you. We'll get through this."

Remember, God's performance-free love doesn't safeguard us from turbulent seasons. It's not a problem-free journey. Where's the witness in that? God doesn't remove the valleys from his kids' lives; he just promises to go with us through them (Psalm 23:3). It's when we grip our Father's hand tightly in life's dark moments, trusting him completely and receiving his peace, that we truly display God's amazing love, unveiling to the world where our hope rests: in the Indestructible One, Jesus Christ, who loves us with his no-matter-what love.

CHAPTER 12

the mural of God's performance-free love

PRACTICING MARRIAGE

"The two will become one flesh."
Jesus, in Matthew 19:5

I can think of no better venue in which to display performance-free love than marriage. Marriage, like no other human relationship, unveils what we really believe when it comes to God and his amazing love for us. If we really have bought into it, we'll find ourselves resonating with Robertson McQuilken's story.

It's a shame many of us don't know his name, but I guess that's kind of his point. For years, Dr. McQuilkin served as the president of Columbia International University in South Carolina. He traveled the world as a representative of the school, could be heard across the nation on a radio show, and was a gifted leader. But all of that ended when Muriel, his beloved wife of more than forty years, was diagnosed with Alzheimer's disease. Sure, there was a period of time when Robertson thought he could continue as a university president while hiring the best caregivers for his ailing wife, but it didn't take long for him to see that Muriel did much better when he was around. So Robertson McQuilkin quit and slipped quietly into the shadows, where for the next several years he cooked Muriel's meals, gave her warm baths, and cared for this woman who increasingly had a hard time remembering him. He did this until her death.

Not long after resigning his prestigious post at CIU, Robertson and Muriel were in an airport waiting for their flight when she suddenly took off running. This had become a bit of a habit in the early days of Muriel's battle with Alzheimer's. She would forget where she was and in a panic start running. On this day, as on other days, Robertson patiently pursued his bride, caught up to her, draped his arm around her, and gently affirmed everything was okay and reminded her how much he loved her. Out of the corner of his eye, Robertson saw a young woman on her computer, muttering something about the two of them. He asked the woman to clarify what she said. "Oh," she replied, "I was just saying to myself that I hope I'll find someone to love me the way you love your wife."

THE MARRIAGE APOCALYPSE

A recent CNN article put words to what you and I already know: We are in the middle of a marriage apocalypse in which millions are giving up on the first institution God created.[1] One of the major reasons for this mass exodus is that we are at a real deficit of "marriage posters," those unions that inspire us to give our lives to someone else under the covenant of marriage—in sickness and in health. It's more than fair to ask, "Where are the modern-day Robertson McQuilkins?"

I'm guessing you have a general grasp on the heartbreaking statistics about marriage and divorce, so there's no need to rehash them. Of all the data, the rapid decline in the marriage rate is most alarming. People are 20 percent less likely to marry today than they were fifty years ago. On one level, this makes sense, especially when we consider there are close to forty-two million Americans who have been married more than once—and of course, this doesn't count those who have been divorced and chose to not remarry. With all this brokenness, why would children of divorce aspire to marriage and make themselves vulnerable to such pain and devastation?

However broken the institution of marriage may be in the white community, the brokenness is significantly higher among African Americans—for understandable and yet inexcusable reasons. Slavery thrived off of the division of families. On the auction block, families were ripped apart—mother sent to one state, father to another, and children to others. This ugly chapter in American history bequeathed to my people a legacy of broken families—a legacy whose seismic tremors we continue to feel today. In his book *Is Marriage for White People?* Dr. Richard Banks writes, "Over the past half century, African Americans have become the most unmarried people in our nation. By far. We are the least likely to marry and the most likely to divorce; we maintain fewer committed and enduring relationships than any other group. Not since slavery have black men and women been as unpartnered as we are now."[2]

While no single ethnicity has a monopoly on broken families, my community has felt and continues to feel its potent sting.

A FAILURE TO LAUNCH

Marriage is significant, sociologists point out, because historically there has been a correlation between the health of a society and the state of its families. Whatever your opinion may be on the relationship between men and women within the marriage covenant, it cannot be dismissed, both historically and theologically, that there's a corresponding relationship between thriving marriages and thriving men. Please don't misunderstand me. I am certainly not saying all marriage dysfunction can be blamed on dysfunctional men. What I—and the statistics—point to is that if we can inspire men to embrace authentic, biblical manhood, we set them, their families, and our society on an upward trajectory of health.

For example, sociologists say we are living in an age of extended adolescence. Adolescence can be defined as wanting the privileges of adulthood without the responsibilities. Researchers tell us that adolescence in America today has actually extended to age thirty-five. Our boys are not growing up. We have a lot of boys trapped in men's bodies, and this is wreaking havoc on marriage and family.

Several years ago, a movie called *Failure to Launch* released. In the movie, we are introduced to a thirtysomething-year-old "man" still living at home with his parents, completely devoid of ambition. His mother cooks for him and does his laundry. He is clueless about the quiet frustration his parents endure as they secretly wish their child would find a passion for something and leave their home. Out of desperation, his parents hire a "professional interventionist," who is tasked to motivate their son to leave the nest and get a life. It's more than easy to dismiss *Failure to Launch* as some kind of exaggeration, a Hollywood distortion of reality, but my years as a pastor coming face-to-face with young "men," as depicted in this movie, tells me the film is disturbingly real, with its finger on the pulse of a national pandemic: adolescent boys trapped in men's bodies.

What does all of this have to do with marriage? Everything. While the marriage rate is declining, the cohabitation rate is increasing. "Shacking up," as some call it, actually appeals to the adolescent mind-set. "So I can have the privileges of marriage without the responsibilities? Sounds good to me! I'm all in!" As one comedian pointed out in an all-too-honest moment,

"Boys play house; men make homes." Marriage really is for grown folks, so what happens when people are chronologically aging but stuck in the teenage years emotionally? We have the marriage apocalypse.

THE REAL CULPRIT

One of the major ways to manifest God's performance-free love is to walk in relationship with others—and, of course, there's no better relationship for sharing God's performance-free love than marriage. If we could ever pinpoint a time and setting for something that is not transactional or quid pro quo, it's in our marriages today. Sadly, marriage for many has become a perpetual audition in which we force our spouses to prove their worth—and if we become unhappy or disgruntled, we look for the exits. Marriage in the twenty-first century has proven to be anything but indestructible.

One of life's biggest challenges is to connect with people in rich, meaningful ways over a prolonged period of time. Community is our greatest longing and yet our severest challenge. People can be frustrating, and many of our relationships have been huge disappointments. Who hasn't endured the trauma of a failed relationship? *What happened to this friendship?* we wonder. *We used to be so close, but now we no longer speak.* How did the couple go from "JUST MARRIED!" sprayed on their wedding-day car to sighing, "Just . . . married," to filing for divorce? In many cases, our relationships expire when we are no longer happy. All too often, I'm forced to confront a horrid hypocrisy in my relationships with others: I long for a performance-free love, but I'm not as prone to extend this to others. Our relationships have an expiration date when they become a venture in transactional happiness. This is the real culprit behind the marriage apocalypse.

In Matthew 19, Jesus is approached by religious leaders and asked a volatile question: "Is it lawful for a man to divorce his wife for any and every reason?" (verse 3). At the heart of the inquiry was a standing debate between two streams of Jewish thought. On one end stood the followers of Shammai, a Jewish rabbi who taught that the only reason to divorce was unfaithfulness—specifically, sexual unfaithfulness. At the other end of the spectrum was the school of Hillel, who taught a more liberal outlook on marriage and divorce, saying a man could divorce his wife for any and every reason. For example, if she disrespected him or wore her hair down in public (a cultural sign of immodesty), he could divorce her. If his wife burned the food or could be heard talking inside her house by neighbors, he could divorce her. I wish I was making this up, but I'm not.

I'll give you three guesses on which view had the most followers—and the first two don't count. You got it—Hillel, whose happiness outlook on marriage won the day. The philosophical undercurrent to his teachings on marriage and divorce was fundamentally how marriage was about the happiness and satisfaction of the husband. If at whatever point the husband no longer felt happy, he could leave.

While we're thousands of years removed from the teaching of Hillel, we still feel its effects on our culture. "Life, liberty, and *the pursuit of happiness*" is the gravitational pull we all feel, and the moment our marriages don't make us happy, our eyes tend to look elsewhere.

David Brooks, *New York Times* writer and author of *The Road to Character*, diagnoses how we've devolved into a "happiness at all costs" society. The problem, as Brooks sees it, actually begins in the aftermath of what Tom Brokaw called "the greatest generation"—the generation of Americans who sacrificed their lives in World War II. While we don't need to idolize them or the past—they were, after all, the generation of Jim Crow—they were a selfless lot who paid a great price. Not long after returning from the war, they decided they had paid their dues and it was time to enjoy the fruits of their labor. So en masse they moved out of cities and into suburbs. While we don't know their parenting philosophies, we do know their children (Baby Boomers) ushered in the drugs era and sexual revolution and broadcasted a message of strong individualism. Sure, some of their causes were just, but what becomes clear among the children of the "greatest generation" is a rigid commitment to the pursuit of happiness. And the statistics unveil an ugly truth: It's precisely at this moment that marriage begins to take a downward turn for the worse.

REDEEMING MARRIAGE

Normally, we would expect Jesus, when cornered by two opposing groups with a question, to masterfully wiggle his way out by offering a completely original, new way of thinking about the issue at hand. And while he does this numerous times in the gospels, it isn't the case in Matthew 19. Jesus unashamedly takes sides by standing with the school of Shammai: "I tell you that anyone who divorces his wife, except for sexual immorality, and marries another woman commits adultery" (verse 9). Jesus vehemently opposes any outlook on marriage that ventures into the covenant with individual happiness at the forefront.

Why is Jesus so strong in his opposition to a happiness worldview of marriage? Because Jesus understands that any transactional approach to human relationships sees the other in purely utilitarian means, thus dehumanizing them in the process. I'm sure you picked up on this as we looked at several reasons for divorce given by Rabbi Hillel. Who held all the cards? The men. How were the women pictured in the covenant of marriage? As nothing more than sexual instruments existing for the pleasure of their husbands. For those who saw the 1980s cult classic *Coming to America*, Prince Akeem's proposed bride at the beginning of the movie was nothing more than an instrument cultivated from birth solely for the pleasure of her prince. So in a shameless scene, she jumps up and down on one foot, barking like a dog, affirming that her existence is to totally commit herself to whatever he likes. In this marriage worldview, the husband becomes deity, and the woman less than humanity. Both extremes are outside of God's vision for marriage. What's more, when anyone approaches marriage from the vantage point of their fulfillment and happiness, are they not positioning themselves as God?

So how do we redeem marriage, the first institution God created? Jesus shows us the way forward. His answer to the religious leaders' question takes them on a scriptural journey back to the roots of marriage in Genesis 2. With a statement laced with righteous sarcasm, Jesus begins his answer by saying, "Haven't you read . . .?" and then he quotes God's instructions for marriage from the sacred Scriptures.

The religious leaders had let marriage deteriorate to a cultural war between two divergent worldviews and interpretations on marriage. Notice Jesus' answer to their question does not begin with their worldview, but with God's as found in the Scriptures. His "haven't you read . . .?" followed by a recitation of Genesis 2 is critical in our quest to redeem marriage, showing how we must begin with the transcendent truth of the Bible.

Marriage is God's idea—his product, best done his way. Marriage is not the fruit of a governmental constitution, nor is it to be left to the interpretation of a group of judges trying to parse the intended or literal meaning of the authors of the constitution.

Marriage is a biblical ideal flowing from the words of a living God. If we have any hope of redeeming marriage, we must follow Jesus' example and appeal to the Scriptures as our sole guide.

Jesus points out that marriage is not the product of two people deciding to take each other for a test-drive to see if they can make each other happy. Instead, marriage is a sovereign union in which husband and wife are yoked together by a holy God. Talk about a game changer. If God put Korie and me together on July 3, 1999, then there must be a loftier vision for marriage than my hedonistic dreams. One Christian book on marriage wonders aloud if marriage is ultimately not about our happiness but our holiness.[3] Certainly, when done God's way, marriage makes us better, but this approach, while noble, still doesn't get to the aim of marriage. See, if I look at Korie and say, "She's going to make me more like Jesus," isn't this still a highly utilitarian and selfish approach to the covenant of marriage?

More than our happiness and holiness, marriage is about the glory of God. The Hebrew word for marriage (*kiddushin*) means "consecration." To consecrate something carries with it the idea of to "set aside" or to "set apart." When anything was consecrated in the Scriptures, God was saying it was different, unique, uncommon. Now God isn't into things being different for the sake of being different or cool. To be set apart was for a purpose—and that purpose was to reflect the glory of God. This is why the book of Leviticus, with its statutes and ordinances, was written. Interspersed between what feels like minute laws is the word *holy* (which has the idea of "to consecrate"). The purpose for all the laws was for Israel—in a land surrounded by pagan nations that held a lot in common, such as the worship of many gods—to stand apart. These nations were to look at Israel and say "different," and what made them different was the God they served.

This is marriage. God wants our unions to stand apart. He's setting your home and my home like a city on a hill, to shine as a light in a dark culture fractured by broken homes and in a generation that has thrown their hands in the air and is giving up on the institution en masse. As it was with Robertson McQuilkin with Muriel, so God wants it to be for us—with our marriages being beacons that infuse hope into a depleted world. More than about my happiness or your holiness, marriage is about God's glory.

One of my childhood friends grew up in a broken home. We met as little boys in church, and decades later, I've still never set eyes on his dad—only his mom. Growing up, he was always at our house, sitting at our dinner table and watching ball games. Recently, he and his wife went through a turbulent time in their marriage—so turbulent that my friend decided to leave. The cycle of brokenness looked like it was only going to continue. As he was packing his things, a book fell out of his bag. It happened to be a book written by my dad. He picked it up, and his mind took him back to our dinner table on the south side of Atlanta. He recalled all those family devotions. The scene of my dad loving my mom was too much. He unpacked his possessions, decided to dig in, and reached out to my dad to thank him. In my parents, he had found his marriage poster and fresh inspiration.

I can tell you from firsthand experience that Mom and Dad do not have a problem-free marriage. They have buried a daughter and felt the suffocating pain of ministry. We children tested them tremendously. There have been many seasons where if the vitality of their marriage had been anchored in the happiness the other provided, divorce would have been a welcomed option, I'm sure. We've all been there. What has sustained my parents is the sense that someone is watching them. Crawford and Karen Loritts had the feeling that people were taking in their union from far and wide. God had consecrated them as a beacon of hope to a world, a society, and even an ethnicity that has been particularly ravaged by the marriage apocalypse.

A RECIPROCAL JOY

If the chapter ended here, I could see the reader viewing marriage as if it were merely some manual labor job we clock in at every day—because, after all, *We have to put food on the table, and there's a responsibility to bear. So let's just grin and bear it, and somehow, some way, we'll get through it.* This is an inaccurate picture of marriage. God is for us and for our joy, and he wants us to experience this same joy as we enter and abide in the marriage covenant.

When two people who are experiencing God's performance-free love marry, a very interesting thing happens: Life becomes about the glory of God together, sharing this amazing love with each other and fulfilling his purposes. As this happens, I find God is for my being used by him to delight my spouse, and as my spouse finds joy through my devotion to God and to her, she reciprocates.

In his book *Love and Respect*, Emerson Eggerichs argues that a man's fundamental felt need is respect, while a wife's is to feel loved. When one does not have this need met, the other will respond to their spouse's failure to perform by withholding their spouse's felt need. So when a husband doesn't feel respected, he will not provide love in tangible ways to his wife; and when a wife doesn't feel loved, she will withhold respect. It's what Eggerichs calls "the crazy cycle."[4] In order to derail the crazy cycle, he says one spouse needs to meet the other spouse's felt need, even when theirs is not being met. This takes a level of sacrifice foreign to most, and it's here that the gospel offers hope.

Marriage only works the way God intends when both husband and wife rely on God to serve their spouses in ways that bring happiness and fresh joy to their souls. What made Robertson McQuilkin exchange the public platform of his office for years of ambiguity, serving his beloved Muriel when she didn't even recognize him enough to say thank you? It's the gospel. Joy is found when I experience God's supernatural, performance-free love, and out of sheer delight and joy, I'm inspired and strengthened to share that love with my spouse.

This is what Scott Sauls, senior pastor at Christ Presbyterian Church in Nashville, calls the upside-down nature of the kingdom. Joy in Christ is not found when I try to find it independent of him. Instead, joy—real joy—is only discovered when I selflessly live for him through the power he provides. Joy awaits in marriage when I live for the joy of my spouse.

THE RESTORATION OF HUMANITY

When marriage is redeemed by living for the glory of God and for the joy of my spouse, I am not only positioned to receive joy in marriage; at the same time, I return to my spouse the dignity of her humanity. Korie is no longer a tool used for my delight. She becomes truly more than a cook, maid, or object. Instead, Korie is seen as being on an equal footing with me as my bride and friend.

In the twenty-first century, this is nothing new, but to the first-century world—the world of Jesus—this was a shocking concept. In almost every culture in Jesus' day, women were regarded as pieces of property and inferior to men. The most common occupation of a divorced woman was prostitution—the only place to which she could turn financially in that era's sexist times.

So along comes Jesus, who reaches all the way back to Genesis 2 and reminds the religious leaders, "'For this reason a man will leave his father and mother and be united to his wife, and the two will become one flesh.' So they are no longer two, but one flesh" (Matthew 19:5–6). Marriage involves the man uniting to his bride, which is what some call cleaving. This phrase has the fragrance of value and honor. The apostle Peter picked up on this: "Likewise, husbands, live with your wives in an understanding way, showing honor to the woman as the weaker vessel, since they are heirs with you of the grace of life, so that your prayers may not be hindered" (1 Peter 3:7 ESV).

A lot has been made of the phrase "weaker vessel." It's a real blemish on the Christian record that a lot of men have used this phrase to argue in error for the superiority of men, but nothing could be further from the truth. I believe "weaker vessel" argues in another direction.

In your home, you have several different vessels you drink from. My guess is some are plastic. These are rugged vessels. Throw them down, and nothing will happen. And then, if you're like me, you may have a special case that houses your most precious drinking vessels. Maybe they're made out of crystal or some fine yet fragile material. These vessels are in one sense weaker, but ultimately they are more valuable. You handle them with care because they are precious to you. Peter is using this latter meaning when referring to married women. Think of the context in which he makes this statement. To argue for the preciousness and value of women in the first-century world was astounding. The only place you could hear this and see it practiced was the church.

Marriage in the way God pronounced and Jesus proclaimed involves the restoring of humanity to our spouse. No longer a tool who exists to buy things or provide shelter and security, our spouse is now elevated from the utilitarian to the human.

FOR BETTER, FOR WORSE, NO MATTER WHAT

When two people embark on the journey of marriage, they embrace the mission of a lifetime of coming together in what Jesus calls "one flesh." The physical union we share in marriage is an illustration of the comprehensive union we are to experience. God designed sex in marriage for both spouses to communicate to each other, "I see the best and the worst of you, and I still want you." This is truly performance-free love. This is what it means to be one. As my friend Tim Downs says, "Oneness in marriage is soul-level harmony." Tim Keller, in his book *The Meaning of Marriage*, suggests this concept points to friendship in the deepest, truest, most intimate of ways.[5] When husband and wife plumb the depths and scale the peaks of friendship with each other, they not only give back to each other joy and humanity, but they also experience an indestructible union.

My grandparents were married for more than fifty-three years. While they were both devoted to Christ, their marriage experienced trials along the way. There was the pressure of marriage in the Jim Crow South and its persistent chipping away at human dignity. There was the stress of leaving the South to start a new life together up north, and later in life, there were health crises, such as heart surgeries, high blood pressure, and so on. Yet through it all, they stayed together and became an inspiring poster of marriage. I'm just seventeen years in, and I pray I can have what they had.

Toward the end of my grandfather's life, he was beset with health challenges. One night, my dad was sleeping in the other room, having come to town to visit and tend to some business for them. In the middle of the night, he heard my grandfather moan and apologize to my grandmother: "I'm sorry, Sylvia; I tried." Evidently, my grandfather had to go to the bathroom pretty bad, but he couldn't move fast enough, so he made a mess. Scurrying to her feet to clean up after him, my grandmother said, "That's all right, Crawford. I'll clean it up. We're married." My nana's behavior wasn't predicated on his performance or lack thereof; in some sense, it was only beautified by it.

This is the indestructible marriage. It's performance-free. It's removing the fig leaves and letting each other in on the most intimate and vulnerable levels. The indestructible marriage says we are in this, no matter what: "I'll clean it up. We're married."

saved from ourselves

A WAY OUT OF
CRUSHING PERFORMANCE

Some of America's most elite and prestigious universities are experiencing an uptick in cases of depression and suicide among their students. This is a real head-scratcher. I would think the depressed and suicidal would be found among those who *didn't* get in, not those who did. In a recent *New York Times* article, an Ivy League student at the University of Pennsylvania named Kathryn DeWitt was profiled:

> As the elder child of a civil engineer and preschool teacher in San Mateo, Calif., Ms. DeWitt, now 20, has understood since kindergarten that she was expected to attend an elite college . . .
>
> [Once there] she awoke daily at 7:30 a.m. and often attended club meetings until as late as 10:00 p.m. She worked 10 hours a week as part of her financial aid package, and studied furiously, especially for her multivariable calculus class. Would she never measure up? Was she doing enough? Was she taking full advantage of all the opportunities?[1]

But then, the article detailed, she bombed her calculus midterm. The grade was so poor that she feared she would fail the class altogether. This one single test score, in DeWitt's mind, was going to end her future plans to teach math before they ever had a chance to get started.

> "I had a picture of my future, and as that future deterio-rated," she said, "I stopped imagining another future." The pain of being less than what she thought she ought to be was unbearable. The only way out, she reasoned with the twisted logic of depression, was death."[2]

Kathryn DeWitt represents a growing dilemma on our university campuses: high performers who are at the same time unfulfilled to the point of depression and even entertaining thoughts of suicide. More proof that a white-knuckled performance ethic won't quite scratch us where our soul itches.

I remember years ago, stumbling across a line in Solomon's dark memoir, the book of Ecclesiastes: "I undertook great projects: I built houses for myself and planted vineyards"—and then came these words: "Yet when I surveyed all that my hands had done and what I had toiled to achieve, everything was meaningless, a chasing after the wind" (Ecclesiastes 2:4, 11). When Solomon remarked that he took on some great projects, it's sort of like Bill Gates saying he's made a few dollars; it's a bit of an understatement. Solomon built the temple of God, one of the seven wonders of the ancient world. Talk about an achievement. Yet, just as it was for Kathryn DeWitt, it's almost impossible to ignore the depressed, melancholy tone behind his words. There's no joy. No gladness. It's as though Solomon looks at the temple he built, shrugs his shoulders, and walks away.

Let's be honest. Hard work. Performance. It's never about just hard work or performance. You're after something beyond the striving. For Kathryn, it was about earning the approval of her parents. For Solomon, it was about becoming the greatest person ever to walk the face of the earth. For me, as I told you at the beginning of this book, it was about earning my own approval and getting out from under my dad's shadow. What is it for you? What are you trying to earn in your own strength?

No matter what it looks like for you, we all need a way out of this kind of life-draining striving and straining.

GOING TO WAR WITH THE MERITOCRACY

Here's what we know: We live in a meritocracy that makes value judgments on people based on their accomplishments, talent, work, and the number of accolades they receive for such work. The flip side, of course, is that our world also makes value judgments on our *lack* of any of these things.

Even worse, this culture of meritocracy has crept into our churches. Friends, it has crept into our very souls. All of us in our own ways have been trying to save ourselves.

The gospel of Matthew is the good news written to good people like us to whom Jesus says tenderly, "You can stop your trying now. You can drop the performance. Put it all aside—do you feel that burden lifting?—and come, abide in me."

Easier said than done, I know. Tomorrow you will wake up and feel the gravitational pull of our society beckoning you to prove yourself yet again. This is not the way of Jesus. Every day is a fight for us to go from striving to abiding, from performing to being. This fight is exactly what it is—a knock-down, drag-out fight. And we're going to have to go after the pull of the meritocracy with the same intensity of a boxer training for his next opponent.

Insecurity is one of the accomplices in a performance-driven life. When a person doesn't feel intrinsically accepted for who they are, they'll inevitably reach for their "dancing shoes." So we'll work harder; obsess to unhealthy proportions over grades, money, or relationships; or try as hard as we can to gain God's approval by being good. This is just the way of the meritocracy. But God offers a completely different way, and if we can ever learn to rest in his love and approval, we will have dealt a fatal blow to the beast of meritocracy.

RESTING IN THE FATHER'S LOVE

In Matthew 3:17, we hear God say of Jesus, "This is my Son, whom I love; with him I am well pleased." Earlier we pointed out that these words from God came *before* Jesus had done any miracles—before he had calmed the seas, opened blinded eyes, or died on a cross. God wanted his Son to know, *You are loved, regardless of what you do.* These words are repeated in Matthew 17:5 when Jesus is transfigured on the mountain. And all throughout his life, Jesus returns to his Father in prayer time and time again, resting in his love.

I remember sitting in a movie theater, being immersed in the life of Amy Winehouse. As I watched this documentary, I had the same feeling as when I watched *Titanic* for the first time—I knew it ended badly, but I was naively hopeful I was wrong.

Amy Winehouse was a once-in-a-generation talent. Her voice was compared to Billie Holiday's—and ultimately her life would be as well. For all her success, Amy was a miserable soul. After eating, she quietly retreated to bathrooms to expel her latest meal. Amy battled alcoholism and drugs. Despite all of the praise and accolades, she seemed to become more uncomfortable and miserable the more she was adored by the masses. Performance didn't bring her fulfillment; in a weird sort of way, it only heightened the emptiness. But where did this emptiness come from? In a telling scene, Amy talks about the day her parents divorced and her dad walked out. I fought to hold back tears as she said that something in her died when her dad left. We don't need a degree in psychology to piece together Amy's problems—with no secure love from a father, Amy was left profoundly empty and vulnerable.

Amy's story is a familiar one. Another troubled performer, Tupac Shakur sang about how at his dad's passing, his anger wouldn't let him "feel for a stranger."[3] Like Amy Winehouse, Tupac died young, spending his few brief moments on earth grasping for the security and significance a loving, present father should have given him.

Maybe this hits a little too close to home. You know Amy's and Tupac's pain. You have no category for the words, "This is my child, whom I love; with her I am well pleased," because, well, you've never heard them. So could it be that your obsession with work, relationships, or good deeds is your attempt to find someone or something to say those words to you?

Life in the meritocracy tends to be all about me and my attempts to find value and love through, well, my attempts. So off we go, trying to ascend "Mount Significance" through our own efforts, hoping to catch greatness along the way. But what if I told you there's a completely different way, a counterintuitive path? What if I showed you that the great God who created you and me not only relieves us of our strivings to find love and acceptance through our performance, but also delights in taking average people like us and making us great simply by being in relationship with him?

Of all the things written in this book, you need to really hear this. I want to speak words of life over you. The same God who said to his Son, Jesus, "This is my Son, whom I love; with him I am well pleased," is the same God who stands ready to save and adopt you into his family. And if you are his child, he says to you, "You are my child, whom I love; with you I am well pleased." These words of love, acceptance, and security have nothing to do with your performance. God doesn't take them back after a one-night stand. He doesn't regret saying them after the lie, the morsel of gossip, the self-destructive choices, or the cheating no one knows about but you. Instead, he says, "You are my child. I'm proud of you. You don't ever have to perform for me to get me to love and accept you." End of story. Of course God wants us to confess and trust him to wash and change us; these are not things *we do to gain* his love, but these are things *we do in response* to his amazing, performance-free love for us.

Isn't this amazing news? You don't have to perform for his love—you already have it. Jesus went to war on the meritocracy *for you*, to save you from all the posturing, all the perfectionism seeking, all the exhausting, endless trying to make it on your own. This is the heart of the gospel of Matthew, and its message is just as true for you and me today: Jesus is the true Savior of those who will never be "good enough" to save themselves.

What a relief! We can drop the performing act and simply abide. This is exactly Jesus' invitation to you and me today.

A NEW WAY FORWARD

I was having lunch with my dad some time ago, and my ears perked up when he said he was making some changes to his will. I naturally inquired what those changes were. He didn't tell me, but he did mention how his lawyer noticed he had four kids— three biological and one adopted. He told my father how state law stipulated that at any given point, my dad could remove one of his biological kids from his will, but at no time could the status of his adopted child be amended. My adopted sibling is secure.

The Bible says when a person comes to faith in Jesus Christ and accepts his performance-free grace, they have been adopted into the family of God (Ephesians 1:5) and sealed with God's Holy Spirit. We're secure. Adoption is not second-class citizenship; it's first-class security.

So put away your try-harder tactics and rest in the Father's love. When you sin, tell yourself you've been adopted into the family and God has no thoughts of removing you. The meritocracy is alive and active, and while it may try to trip you up, remember *who you are* in Jesus Christ and the truth he says about you that in him, you are enough. In him, you will find the life you want most—a life vibrant with a future hope, an unshakeable love, and a transcendent purpose. And guess what? You don't have to earn it. In fact, you can't. It's all a gift.

Jesus is inviting you to stop performing for him and to start abiding in him. No matter what, God's declaration to his Son, Jesus, is exactly what he says to you and me today: "This is my child, whom I love; with you I am well pleased."

Now *that* is very good news.

acknowledgments

This book was written during an intense time of unsettledness. I had just resigned from Fellowship Memphis to transition to Trinity Grace in New York City. However, we needed to wait until our kids got out of school, and as we waited, we also needed to begin the process of packing and getting our house ready to sell. My bride, Korie, graciously allowed me pockets of time during the day to steal away and write. Without her generosity, this book would not have happened. Korie, you are God's greatest gift to me—outside of salvation.

Parenting has been my favorite professor when it comes to instructing me in the ways of God. Through my many failures, God mercifully unveils sides of himself that oftentimes run counter to how I treat my own children. Quentin, Myles, and Jaden—Daddy is trying to show you the same type of love God shows us. I say to you what God said to his own Son, Jesus, and what he says to you daily: "You are my sons, whom I love; with you I am well pleased." This book encompasses my hopes and dreams for you. May you rest in your heavenly Father's love.

Andrew Wolgemuth and I have enjoyed a rich partnership for almost a decade. I often tell people that Andrew is a godly man with a passion for Jesus, the multiethnic church, and the orphan, and he is also a wise literary agent who helps me navigate the tension between ministry and business. God has used you tremendously in my life, and I hope we enjoy a sustained and fruitful partnership.

Danielle Ridley has been monumental in helping me steward efficiently the ministry God has entrusted to me. When Korie and I followed God's leading to Trinity Grace, I kindly asked my new church to bring Danielle on board, and they graciously accepted—she's been that vital. Her administrative excellence enables me to preach and write with clarity. Whatever way God has used me over the almost ten years we've served together is in large part due to her. Thanks, Danielle!

This book is my first offering as part of the Zondervan family, and it's been a dream come true. Many of the authors I've long admired have spent some part of their careers with Zondervan, so when we locked arms for this project, I was, well, giddy. Stephanie Smith—you were a joy to work with, and I am deeply grateful to you for your insight and patience, as you've played a critical role in the editorial process.

notes

INTRODUCTION: REVOLUTION AGAINST THE MERITOCRACY

1. Randy Alcorn, *Heaven* (Wheaton, IL: Tyndale, 2004), xix.
2. Viktor Frankl, *Man's Search for Meaning* (New York: Touchstone, 1984), 70.

CHAPTER 1: SOUL SONGS

1. Frederick Douglass, *Narrative of the Life of Frederick Douglass* (Mineola, NY: Dover, 1995), 9.
2. From the motion picture *Chariots of Fire*, produced by David Puttnam, directed by Hugh Hudson, written by Colin Welland.
3. Walter Isaacson, *Steve Jobs* (New York: Simon and Schuster, 2011), 425.

CHAPTER 2: MY JESUS MERCY

1. See the discussion in C. S. Lewis, *Mere Christianity* (New York: Macmillan, 1960), 109–12.
2. Francis A. Schaeffer, *No Little People* (Wheaton, IL: Crossway, 2004), 49.
3. R. Albert Mohler Jr., "Moralistic Therapeutic Deism—the New American Religion," *Christian Post* online, April 18, 2005, www.christianpost.com/news/moralistic-therapeutic-deism-the-new-american-religion-6266/ (accessed December 10, 2015).

4. Mahatma Gandhi, *An Autobiography: The Story of My Experiments with Truth* (Boston: Beacon, 1957), 136.

5. Ibid., 124–25.

CHAPTER 3: A GOOD IMPOSSIBILITY

1. Leon Morris, *The Gospel according to Matthew*, Pillar New Testament Commentary (Grand Rapids: Eerdmans, 1992), 91.

CHAPTER 4: ANAMORPHIC PRIDE

1. C. S. Lewis, *Mere Christianity* (New York: Macmillan, 1960), 108–9.

2. Ibid., 109.

3. Ibid.

CHAPTER 7: GRILLED GRACE

1. See Robert J. Schreiter, *The Ministry of Reconciliation: Spirituality and Strategies* (Maryknoll, NY: Orbis, 1998), 109.

2. See Edward Gilbreath, *Reconciliation Blues: A Black Evangelical's Inside View of White Christianity* (Downers Grove, IL: InterVarsity, 2006).

CHAPTER 9: THE MOST DIFFICULT MATH PROBLEM IN THE WORLD

1. Timothy Keller, *The Reason for God: Belief in an Age of Skepticism* (New York: Dutton, 2008), 188–91.

2. Cited in Nelson Mandela, *No Future Without Forgiveness* (New York: Doubleday, 1999), 272.

3. Ibid., 31.

4. Ibid., 129–30.

5. Ibid., 104.

6. Ibid., 35.

7. Ibid., 28, 120, 212.

CHAPTER 10: THE INDICATOR LIGHT OF THE KINGDOM

1. Charles Edward White, "What Wesley Practiced and Preached about Money," *Leadership* (Winter 1987), www.christianitytoday.com/le/1987/winter/87l1027.html (accessed March 22, 2016).

2. Ron Sider, *The Scandal of the Evangelical Conscience: Why Are Christians Living Just Like the Rest of the World?* (Grand Rapids: Baker, 2005), 21, 118–19.

CHAPTER 11: GOD'S GOT YOU

1. John Piper, "Every Moment in 2013 God Will Be Doing 10,000 Things in Your Life," DesiringGod.org, January 1, 2013, www.desiringgod.org/articles/every-moment -in-2013-god-will-be-doing-10-000-things-in-your-life (accessed March 3, 2016).

2. Stephen Plant, *Bonhoeffer* (New York: Continuum, 2004), 136.

CHAPTER 12: THE MURAL OF GOD'S PERFORMANCE-FREE LOVE

1. Carol Costello, "The Marriage Apocalypse May Be Coming," *CNN.com*, April 7, 2015, www.cnn.com/2015/ 04/07/opinions/costello-marriage-millennials (accessed March 22, 2016).

2. Ralph Richard Banks, *Is Marriage for White People? How the African American Marriage Decline Affects Everyone* (New York: Dutton, 2011), 2.

3. Gary Thomas, *Sacred Marriage: What If God Designed*

Marriage to Make Us Holy More Than to Make Us Happy? (Grand Rapids: Zondervan, 2000, 2015).

4. Dr. Emerson Eggerichs, *Love & Respect: The Love She Most Desires, the Respect He Desperately Needs* (Nashville: Nelson, 2004), 6.

5. Timothy Keller, *The Meaning of Marriage* (New York: Dutton, 2011), 120–21.

CHAPTER 13: SAVED FROM OURSELVES

1. Julie Sceflo, "Suicide on Campus and the Pressure of Perfection," *New York Times*, August 2, 2015, www.nytimes.com/2015/08/02/education/edlife/stress-social-media-and-suicide-on-campus.html (accessed March 3, 2016).

2. Ibid.

3. Tupac Shakur, "Dear Mama," from the album *Me against the World*, February 1995.